Never Turn Away

Never Turn Away

The Buddhist Path Beyond Hope and Fear

Rigdzin Shikpo

Foreword by Francesca Fremantle

Edited by David Hutchens

WISDOM PUBLICATIONS • BOSTON

Wisdom Publications, Inc.
199 Elm Street
Somerville MA 02144 USA
www.wisdompubs.org

Library of Congress Cataloging-in-Publication Data
Shikpo, Rigdzin.
  Never turn away: the Buddhist path beyond hope and fear / Rigdzin
Shikpo ; foreword by Francesca Fremantle ; edited by David Hutchens.
    p. cm.
  Includes index.
  ISBN 0-86171-488-1 (pbk. : alk. paper)
  1. Four Noble Truths. 2. Spiritual life—Buddhism. I. Fremantle,
Francesca. II. Hutchens, David, 1958– III. Title.
  BQ4230.S55 2007
  294.3'42—dc22
                              2007021083

11 10 09 08 07
5 4 3 2 1

Cover design by Mary Ann Smith. Interior design by Gopa & Ted2, Inc.
Set in Sabon 10/15. Cover photograph by Monte Nagler/Getty Images.

Wisdom Publications' books are printed on acid-free paper and meet the
guidelines for permanence and durability of the Production Guidelines for
Book Longevity of the Council on Library Resources.

Printed in the United States of America

This book was produced with environmental mindfulness. We have
elected to print this title on 50% PCW recycled paper. As a result, we
have saved the following resources: 15 trees, 10 million BTUs of energy, 1,298
lbs. of greenhouse gases, 5,388 gallons of water, and 692 lbs. of solid waste.
For more information, please visit our website, www.wisdompubs.org

Contents

Foreword

Never Turn Away is addressed to everyone who has ever asked themselves the fundamental questions about life and death or the meaning of existence. It will take the reader on a journey of exploration, revealing unsuspected aspects of mind and opening up entirely new ways of experiencing the world. It is not just a book about Buddhism or an account of Buddhist beliefs, but an intensely practical guide, which continually relates the theoretical views and the underlying principles of meditation to everyday life. It constantly drives home the message that we must realize truth directly rather than remaining satisfied with conceptual understanding.

These teachings are brought vividly to life in Rigdzin Shikpo's characteristic style, which is very clear, direct, simple, and down to earth. Making inspired connections across the boundaries of Buddhist thought, the techniques described here are linked to the four noble truths, the traditional basis of the Buddha's teaching. For readers new to meditation or to Buddhism, this book will guide them straight to its heart, while it will bring fresh perspectives and illuminating insights even to experienced practitioners.

Rigdzin Shikpo is one of those Western Buddhists whose life-story would seem to confirm the power of karmic connections and the fruit of practice in former lives. Even as a child, when he first heard the story of the Buddha, he felt an immediate attraction, and from the time he began to practice meditation as a young man, his path appears to have been unusually straightforward and free from significant obstacles. He is also unusual in having had the opportunity to study with representatives of all the three main Buddhist *yanas* or vehicles, and thus to acquire a deep practical knowledge of the entire tradition. It is as though he chose to be born in that particular place and at that particular time in order to encounter the people who would help him to fulfill his potential.

Most importantly, when he met his main teacher, Chögyam Trungpa Rinpoche, he was able to enter without hesitation into the very subtle and often misunderstood relationship between guru and disciple. In the practice of Vajrayana, devotion for one's guru is all-important. It is the catalyst that opens the heart of the student and makes possible a true meeting of minds. It calls forth the transforming power that awakens the student's own buddha nature and allows it to blossom fully. Because of the faith and devotion that Rigdzin Shikpo spontaneously manifested, Trungpa Rinpoche was able to entrust him, even at a very early stage, with the most profound teachings of the Nyingma tradition. Subsequently he authorized him to establish the Longchen Foundation in order to preserve and spread them.

Those who are familiar with Trungpa Rinpoche's work, especially in North America, may wonder why he chose to found a separate, and apparently quite different, lineage on the other side of the Atlantic. He himself said he felt that the tradition of Guru Rinpoche was particularly appropriate for Britain, and it was this that he emphasized during his stay here. After his move to America, his method of teaching developed in a different direction in response to the circumstances he encountered. But it cannot be stressed enough that there is absolutely no disagreement between the various aspects of his activity, which all spring from the awakened mind of one of the great bodhisattvas of this age.

A mathematician by training, Rigdzin Shikpo has a precise and penetrating intellect, enriched by a wide range of interests. He is a natural teacher, with a gift for imparting knowledge, responding to questions, and resolving people's difficulties. He also has a poet's sensitivity to language, and has written fine translations from Tibetan, Dharma texts, and original poetry. Above all, he is clearly motivated by the compassion that longs to help suffering sentient beings by showing them the path to liberation.

While he was studying with Trungpa Rinpoche, Rigdzin Shikpo kept very detailed notes of their meetings. He has always been deeply concerned with preserving the accuracy and integrity of this legacy, while at the same time he follows Rinpoche's own example by continually searching for appropriate ways to express Dharma in the contemporary West. Throughout many years of deepening his own practice and increasing his teaching experience, he has developed a series of programs aimed at bringing out the essential meaning of Buddhism, free from many of the cultural overlays that can sometimes make it seem daunting and alien. This is a work still in progress, using his students as guinea pigs, as he often says. He is also greatly inspired by Khenpo Tsultrim Gyamtso Rinpoche, who has encouraged him to express himself boldly and to go beyond traditional forms.

The teachings in this book are drawn from a number of talks given in England and Germany as an introduction to the view and practice of the Longchen Foundation. They express the very core of Rigdzin Shikpo's approach to Dharma, which he calls the "indestructible heart essence." David Hutchens, who has most skillfully edited and arranged this material, is among his earliest students, one of the discerning few who recognized his remarkable qualities from the first.

The practice of openness and awareness described here allows us to see the significance of our ordinary experience, which is normally lost to us in our unquestioning acceptance of the way things seem to be. We take so many things for granted: the reliability of our perceptions, the power of our emotions, the solidity of objects, even the existence of time and place, and we fail to see their illusory nature. We need to learn how to cut through these projections, which obscure the naked reality of our own being and of the universe.

With his own students Rigdzin Shikpo places great emphasis on the importance of personal transmission when receiving any new Dharma text or instruction. So it is perhaps surprising to find that several powerful methods of meditation are openly described here in some detail. As he says, there is nothing secret about them, yet they are "self-secret" in the sense that they will remain mysterious or obscure to those who are not ready to receive them. It would certainly be difficult for anyone to try to follow the course of training outlined in these pages without qualified guidance, and without the support of fellow practitioners. The intention is to spread the awareness of these wonderful teachings more widely, so that those who are inspired by them may look for a suitable teacher. Even for those who are not in a position to do so at the present moment, reading this book will create a connection to the possibility of encountering the right circumstances at some time in the future.

I have known Rigdzin Shikpo as a Dharma brother since the 1970s, but it was not until several years after Trungpa Rinpoche's death that I began to see him in a different light: as someone who is truly following in his guru's footsteps, and so has become a powerful, authentic teacher in his own right. It has been extraordinarily moving and inspiring to witness his development and transformation into a person who lives only for the welfare of others, and in whom the living presence of the dzogchen lineage manifests without hindrance.

When I listen to Rigdzin Shikpo's Dharma talks, I often feel that Trungpa Rinpoche is speaking through him. Although their personalities could hardly be more different, I have no doubt at all that their minds are one. Having the inconceivable good fortune of being a student of both, it is a great privilege to introduce Rigdzin Shikpo's work to a wider public. May this book lead all who read it to realize the truth of their own being.

Francesca Fremantle

Introduction

THIS BOOK is an introduction to the heart essence of the Buddha's Dharma. These teachings are not, however, something
we start with and can then forget about, as we move on to higher things.
They are central to the Buddhist path, from beginning to end. As we proceed along the path, our understanding of the heart essence grows, and
it's the nub of that same heart-essence teaching that is realized at the end.

The path to understanding the heart essence begins with the simple,
basic questions that most of us ask ourselves at one time or another: questions about life, about who we are and what the world is. And this has
nothing to do with being Buddhist or Christian; it has nothing do with
religion at all, except that, in some sense, it is the fundamental essence of
all religions.

Such questions often come up in adolescence. As children we take
things like our homes, parents, and the places we live for granted. In adolescence, our minds become more open and questioning, perhaps because
of the natural disturbance in our thoughts and feelings that happens
around that time. And from that freshness of mind, in the humdrum round
of ordinary life, we begin to question the point of it all.

We ask ourselves these fundamental questions and feel there must be
an underlying truth to discover. And from a Buddhist perspective it is
meaningful to do this; it's not just a question of adolescent naivety and

wishful thinking. But let's suppose you had discovered the answers. Would you be able to say that the true meaning of life is this or that? What kind of truth can we be talking about?

The Buddha said that we are right, there is a truth to discover, and what is more, we can actually discover it for ourselves. But whether the answer is simple or complex, to think that truth can be explained in conceptual terms is to trivialize it, and from a Buddhist perspective, we could never succeed in expressing truth in this way.

Now if this is the case, you might ask why there are there so very many Buddhist texts. They seem to have a lot to say, and surely they must be talking about something! In fact Buddhist texts talk mostly about how to realize the truth. And, while they may sketch out an approximate vision of it, they never claim to describe the truth itself.

To apprehend truth, we need to use another kind of faculty, one that is unfamiliar to most of us, although the ordinary conceptual mind might be considered a distorted version of it. It is this faculty, a kind of direct knowing beyond conceptual frameworks, that supplies the answers to our fundamental questions.

If someone were to ask us for these answers, however, I'm afraid we would have to respond as the Buddha did—with silence. Nevertheless, something is transmitted through the Buddha's "thunderous silence," as it is sometimes called. It is as if the silence speaks. What is transmitted, however, could never be expressed in words. At best, words could provide a hint, an inspiration, or become a springboard toward the truth.

As adults, we have even more reason to consider these fundamental questions. At this stage, we probably find ourselves in somewhat set patterns, either through economic or family necessity, so there is more reason to ask these questions than ever before. Unfortunately, at this point most of us don't have the same openness we had in our youth. Even if we are inspired to continue our search for truth, we may feel that it's impractical, that it behooves us to accept our limitations; and in any case, we don't know how to proceed.

This is all a bit depressing, really. We may not be literally downcast, but this attitude depresses our energy and narrows our vision. We may look around for answers in science, psychology, therapy, or in the various wisdom traditions found across the world, but it's a bit like stabbing in the dark.

In Buddhism we think you have already started off in the wrong way if you take that approach. From a Buddhist perspective, you need to stay with your original inspiration and work with the directness of your own vision. If you decide not to be dulled by the ways of the world into abandoning your questioning, then the truth will never let you alone. It will always be pricking you onward into asking questions about itself. The quest for truth will continually stir within you, and you will never be able to rest until you have completed it.

Obviously, not everyone feels that way all the time. For some of us it comes and goes throughout our lives. For others it can disappear for many years only to resurface in later life. But all those who are genuinely drawn to the Buddhadharma have some feeling of connection with this truth and the need to discover it.

The path of Buddhadharma is the pursuit of truth itself. The most important quality needed for pursuing this path is openness. In order to pursue and preserve our connection with the truth, we need to cultivate the natural openness of heart and mind that enables us to look at things in a fresh, unbiased way. As we get older, we have to cultivate openness in a more deliberate fashion. The openness we then go on to develop goes far beyond the initial quality of openness that prompted us to ask questions in the first place.

The Buddha's Four Noble Truths

This introduction to the path of Buddhadharma is structured according to the Buddha's four noble truths. Each of the four sections of the book introduces a particular training based on one of these truths.

The traditional Sanskrit terms for the four truths are *duhkha, samudaya, nirodha,* and *marga.* The first truth, *duhkha,* is usually translated as "suffering" or "dis-ease." It is a sense that life is an endless problem. The second truth, *samudaya,* is about the cause of *duhkha.* Why does this suffering arise? The third truth is *nirodha,* which means cessation: that having arisen, suffering can be made to cease. And the fourth truth, *marga*, is the path that brings about the cessation of suffering.

My overall presentation owes a great deal to the teachings of Chögyam Trungpa Rinpoche. It may look a bit different from the way these four truths are presented in library reference books, but, in essence, it's the same. My intention is to give you the flavor of Trungpa Rinpoche's presentation of these essential teachings.

The Influence of Chögyam Trungpa Rinpoche

I first met the Tibetan Buddhist meditation teacher Chögyam Trungpa Rinpoche (1939–87) about forty years ago. He was living in England then and was comparatively unknown, although he later became a famous figure. As far as I am concerned, he was—and I have known many great Buddhist teachers over the years—the greatest meditation teacher I've ever encountered. But at that time, he was teaching in quite a small way in Oxford, and it was not difficult to contact him or meet him face to face in a simple, easy way. I felt myself very fortunate to have met him then, and even more so now, in retrospect.

"Well, lucky for you!" you might say. "But this is just a story to me. Even if I can read his books, I didn't have the good fortune to meet this teacher face to face." While this may be true, Trungpa Rinpoche left an indelible impression on his students, and he inspired and fired up everybody so strongly, that there is a great wish to pass on his tradition to others. So in sharing my experience of his teaching with you, I am fulfilling what I feel would have been his wish and what is indeed my own.

This approach to Buddhist practice begins with the quality of openness. As a teacher, Trungpa Rinpoche always emphasized direct experience and mostly had students work with the single instruction of openness. He had various ways of introducing the experience and power of openness. The instruction, however, was usually very simple, and as he would say, "You just have to do it!" You don't need to worry about whether you can do it or not; you just need to go ahead and surrender to the situation, relate to your anger, or whatever else you are doing.

Openness provides the basis for greater awareness in meditation and in everyday life. However, this is just the beginning. It is the combination of openness and awareness together that lays the ground for seeing significance in our experience.

The Experience of Significance

Buddhist insight comes from appreciating what is significant in experience, but this can't be handed to us on a plate; there is no *Book of Significance*. Buddhist texts can merely hint at such things. In the end, we have to discern the significance of our experience for ourselves. We can read about openness, clarity, sensitivity, and so forth, but merely understanding them as words, at an intellectual level, brings little benefit. They have to affect our hearts; they have to affect our guts; they have to hit us in the deepest part of what we are.

For this, we need to get some experience of the raw data of our lives. You might think, "Well, I've got plenty of that already!" Indeed, as Trungpa Rinpoche used to say, we all have plenty of manure to work with in our everyday experience. We don't need to create more manure in order to grow the field of awareness; we have quite enough material. However, it has to be *raw* material.

The trouble is that much of our experience is dressed up. We think it is raw, but it's dressed up with our preconceptions about the world, about others, and about ourselves. Onto the stream of our experience, thoughts, and emotions, we project notions like, "This all shows that I'm a bad person" or, less commonly, "This all shows I'm a good person"; less common because usually we feel there's something wrong with ourselves or the world.

We find it difficult to experience things as they are, without the clothing or overlay of projections. We always try to make situations into something, rather than experiencing them very simply. Over time we develop a number of verbal, emotional, or conceptual responses and ready-made strategies for handling difficult life situations. Often, these involve turning away from things, so, for example, whenever certain subjects come up in conversation, we reject them out of hand. These conceptual weapons and set patterns stand us in good stead, or so we think. But, in fact, they merely allow us to avoid looking too closely at certain aspects of our lives and prevent us from experiencing things clearly.

PART 1. THE PATH OF OPENNESS

& The Truth of Suffering

"Sweet are the uses of adversity,
Which, like the toad, ugly and venomous,
Wears yet a precious jewel in his head;
And this our life, exempt from public haunt,
Finds tongues in trees, books in the running brooks,
Sermons in stones, and good in everything."
—William Shakespeare, *As You Like It*

With the quality of openness, a kind of lightness creeps into the situation. This is the beginning of a new way of looking at the world.

1. Always Turn Toward, Never Turn Away

IF YOU ASKED Trungpa Rinpoche for the essence of the Buddha's teaching, he would say, "It is very simple. It is simply the teaching of openness, complete openness."

Trungpa Rinpoche's approach was simply to be open and to minimize the projections we make on our experience. His great saying was, "Turn towards everything." Even if we don't know what to do, or how to handle a situation, we just turn toward it. What comes to us might be quite painful, but it is always better to turn toward. It is a very simple choice, although it might be a painful choice sometimes. We can either turn toward or we can turn away, and Trungpa Rinpoche said you should *always* turn toward, and *never* turn away.

We may find, having turned toward a situation, that we don't know what to do. That might be embarrassing, but it's an interesting kind of embarrassment.

Empty Handed

A martial arts teacher once explained to me that the word *karate* means to have "an empty hand." We don't need what he called a "secret sword"; in fact, we train to give up all such secret swords. From a Buddhist point of view, we all have a number of secret—and maybe not so secret—swords which we use to handle difficult circumstances, when all we really need is to be empty handed, to come nakedly into situations.

We could almost call this the path of embarrassment. Ordinarily, we free ourselves from embarrassment in difficult situations by having some contrived method up our sleeves. But the only method that really helps, in the end, is simply to turn toward and experience things clearly. We have to overcome the embarrassment of not always knowing how to handle ourselves. We have to let go of our habits, projections, and other easy, familiar devices that don't really work.

We don't need to be especially brave to practice Dharma. It is more like we reach a situation where there is only one road to take; it's almost the wisdom of despair. We have tried everything else, so why not try this? If we thought we had another option, we might not try anything so radical. Maybe we are irritated with our ordinary ways of reacting to situations. Perhaps there is a simpler way of dealing with existence, something more radical than simply "handling" things.

This approach is actually more real than radical. There is something very wholesome about turning toward things completely and openly. It is very sharp and uncontrived and feels genuine in a way that our ordinary projections and ways of handling things never do. But we will never know this unless we do the practice, because we will have nothing to compare it to.

By turning toward situations as openly as possible we get the raw data of our experience. This is just the first stage, but that first stage is crucial, and carries us a long way.

Seeing Things as They Are

The next stage is more at the level of insight. We might discover, for example, that our sense of self is not as solid as we thought. Or we could have some genuine realization of what we dismissively call "just change." Experiencing a moment of non-ego sounds like more of a discovery because it is such an unfamiliar experience. But everyone knows things change. What is there to discover in that? Well, actually there is a great deal to discover, because we have only a conceptual understanding of change. Intellectually, of course, we all know that things change. But we never feel the significance of change in our hearts and in our guts.

It is obvious that ordinary things change. We can see this as we walk into a room and switch on the television, or leave the house to go shopping. We think that this is just how things work, and its significance doesn't hit us. But when our bodies change—especially if the change is dramatic or sudden—then this has a much greater emotional impact. An accident, or sudden discovery that we or someone close to us has a life-threatening disease, feels much more invasive. But again, we often miss its significance. Instead, we think about visiting a doctor; and as our beauty fades, we wonder about face creams. Meanwhile the significance of aging and change still doesn't hit us.

As Buddhist practitioners, we train to see the significance of impermanence at every level: at the seemingly insignificant level of everyday things like shopping and watching television, as much as the dramatic and emotionally compelling level of old age, sickness, and death.

Some people feel Buddhism is pessimistic. But really it is neither optimistic nor pessimistic. It is just seeing things as they are. Buddhist practice is about becoming more open, clear, and sensitive. There is nothing gloomy about that. Of course, this makes our experience clearer and sharper, and we might not like that. We may feel uncomfortable when our seemingly solid world becomes "more transparent" and "not so easily grasped at," as Trungpa Rinpoche used to say. But it is hardly pessimistic to see that the world of our experience is potentially a much brighter, vaster place than we ever thought possible.

It reminds me of being taken to the seaside when I was very small. Looking at the sea for the first time, I burst into tears and ran away. The sea seemed so very big and I was so small. The sea scared me, but that was no reason for pessimism. I was just seeing clearly what was there before me, and I had to overcome my fear with the help of parents and friends.

The Truth of Suffering

The Buddha's first truth, the truth of suffering, is not saying that everything is miserable. It's saying that suffering, or *duhkha,* is inherent in the very nature of existence and in the basic structure of all sentient beings. Now, Western books on Buddhism often give the impression that the Buddha taught this to everyone he met. But evidence suggests that the Buddha would teach very differently if his audience wasn't ready to discover this universal—if hidden—truth of the nature of things.

The term *duhkha* cannot be fully understood by our ordinary idea of suffering. Technically, its meaning has three aspects: the suffering of suffering, the suffering of impermanence and changes and the suffering of the *skandhas.*

The first is fairly easy to understand. Suffering and dissatisfaction are unfair, in the most obvious sense. The fact that we may already be suffering doesn't insure against more suffering. This is what Trungpa Rinpoche described as the "suffering of suffering." The example he gave to me was that having cancer is no insurance against being run down by a car.

The second, more subtle, aspect of suffering is the duhkha of *anitya,* or the suffering of impermanence and change. Sooner or later, due to the dynamic of change, the things we grasp at and want to continue will fall apart. If we cling to them and have a vested interest in their permanence, we will be forever disappointed and will suffer for that reason.

Of course, it could be argued that if we're already suffering, any change in our circumstances would be a good thing. But this is more subtle than our ordinary notions of liking or disliking; it is the fact that the instability, the collapse, and the finishing of things is painful in itself. We wish for stability and permanence, and this is forever denied us, irrespective of whether we are talking about pain or pleasure. It is something we want but can never get.

The third and most subtle kind of suffering is the duhkha of the five *skandhas.* These are the very constituents of our existence: the form of our bodies, our feelings of pleasure and pain, our sense perceptions, the contents of our minds and hearts, and our consciousness. The skandhas are not only the constituents of our personal existence, they also involve our perception of the external world and the things we hold on to in that world.

The extra subtlety here is that the skandhas are themselves a false creation. Since they don't correspond to what is truly there, we find ourselves emotionally involved in false projections and distortions of reality. Our seeming reality is fundamentally false, and we are absorbed into that falseness, which is painful. This is the most subtle kind of duhkha: the suffering of our very existence.

Taken at face value, most of us in the West would dispute the truth of suffering. Not everything in our lives and in the world is suffering. Yes, there is much suffering in the world—both mental and physical—and life is often unsatisfactory. We are not going to live forever, so there is always that uncertainty hovering over us. But on the scale of suffering, some of us seem to suffer less than others, and on occasion, we all rather enjoy ourselves. Of course, we are talking here about something that points to a much deeper level of experience. But while it is all very well to say this, most Western people still can't relate to it.

In traditional cultures, where there is more respect for the Buddhadharma, and the teaching itself has great charisma, people tend to accept the truth of suffering, whether they understand it or not. It has a cultural meaning for them, and they can go on to train to see the truth of it. Lacking that background, we might easily think that Buddhism must be intrinsically depressing and certainly not life-affirming.

Early Western commentators, looking at the first translations of Buddhist texts, sometimes portrayed Buddhism as being negative and pessimistic. I feel there is no point in pressing on that particular nerve. The Buddha's teaching contains many things, and while the nature of duhkha is fundamental, we can let it emerge gradually, if it does. Who knows? Maybe we will find that, in some deep and profound way, life is wonderful after all, even from a Buddhist perspective.

The most important thing is to experience the nature of our worlds as directly as we can. I say "worlds" because our seemingly common world is made up of all of our very different emotions, ideas, and projections. We can at least aspire to become free of notions and projections about how the world should be, and try to experience things as they are.

That simple act of aspiring to be free, to be free insofar as we can be free, is more important than we might think.

Imaginary Barriers

Trungpa Rinpoche decided that the best way to express the Buddha's teaching was in terms of openness. The word *open* has an immediate meaning for us. We speak of people being open or closed. Being closed is associated with claustrophobia and a narrowed outlook or vision. Being open suggests we are open to many different possibilities and ways of thinking and feeling. We are open to others, allowing them to rub up against or even strike us at times, without immediately blocking them off. Openness is a way of learning about the world that enables us to relate to things properly and to act skillfully.

Trungpa Rinpoche occasionally spoke to me about absolute or complete openness. This is something more than openness in the ordinary sense. Rinpoche suggested it was possible to experience the world free of any ego-contrived barriers whatsoever. Moreover, this state of absolute openness is completely natural. We don't have to construct it, or indeed, deconstruct it, as we say these days. We don't have to pull down a burning wall in our minds and hearts. Such walls exist only in our imagination. That imagination, however, is as powerful as a magical enchantment.

Waking from a Spell

The power of our false view of the world is like an enchantment. The great fourteenth-century master Longchen Rabjam spoke of it in these terms. Enchantment is a good word for it. It's as if we are under a spell, or "glamor," that causes us to see things that aren't there and fail to see things that are. This false view makes up the world as we know it.

This spell is not cast upon us by some evil magician; in a sense we create it ourselves. Through our practice of openness and awareness we become convinced that we are under an enchantment. A gradual sense of dis-enchantment—in the positive sense—arises. Now you might think that this would come as a great relief, but not so, unfortunately. The biggest shock often comes as the spell dissolves, and we find ourselves saying, "Where has my world gone?"

Suddenly we realize that the universe is a much vaster place than we ever imagined. We see what a parochial view we had before. We may yowl that we don't want to go there! We don't want it to be so vast and open! But it's just a sign that we need to straighten ourselves out.

Fortunately, it's not fundamentally that difficult. Many others have done so before, and so can we. This is the Buddhist view and the path of openness, which is certainly not pessimistic.

2. Meditation: The Basis of the Path

WHY WOULD anyone want to learn meditation in the first place? Maybe it seems obvious. Couldn't we all do with a quieter life? Things can get quite rough out there! There are so many things we have to relate to, whether we like it or not. Our jobs, relationships, families, and friends sometimes give us satisfaction, even inspiration, but often they just make us feel trapped. So we look to meditation to get a quieter, calmer mind.

But it isn't as easy as we think. There is no magic wand for calming the mind. When we put a lot of effort into calming the mind it rebels, creating yet another problem. The trouble with always wanting a quiet mind is that sooner or later we get ruffled by circumstances, and should we get sufficiently disturbed, we probably feel our practice is a complete failure.

In formless meditation we take a different approach. Meditation is not about creating a blank mind or suppressing thoughts. The arising and passing away of thoughts isn't an obstruction to meditation. It is a way of learning about our minds. It's a way of appreciating just how powerful our minds are.

It is common knowledge that meditation plays a central part in the lives of Buddhist practitioners. What is less well understood is that meditation, by itself, is not necessarily helpful. Yes, many people are helped by meditation, but often it only has a mild effect for a short while and little overall impact. Sometimes people are even harmed by it.

The problem is that meditation can powerfully reinforce our world view. Our ordinary view is limited by our conditioning, so when we sit down to practice we are meditating within our own confusion. That is why it is important to adopt the right view to start with; one that at least moves us in the right general direction.

Beginning with the Right View

Meditation is most powerful and effective when we start with the right kind of view. View, in this sense, is a way of seeing that leads to a deeper understanding of the nature of experience, rather than holding a particular dogma or set of beliefs. Our ordinary worldview is something that we adopt almost without knowing it. In this view we want to be secure, to establish ourselves in a position where we can't be disturbed. Consequently, we approach meditation as a way to create some calmness and stability of mind.

In contrast, the Buddhist view is an attitude of complete openness toward whatever arises in our minds and daily lives. Through openness we never say "no" to any experience; it allows us to feel everything as completely as we can. Meditating with this view makes us become much more stable and true to ourselves than trying to be calm ever could.

Bringing an attitude of openness to everything we experience is the most important thing we can do. It empowers our meditation and makes it effective. And it helps to develop a robustness of mind that can work with any circumstance that arises.

Openness relates to what Buddhists call *prajna,* or wisdom. It has been a central part of Buddhist training for centuries and helps us to develop as truly human beings.

Openness as the Touchstone

Openness has a flavor to it that sounds appealing. We may well feel that the "complete openness" Trungpa Rinpoche talked about is beyond our reach at the moment. But we can at least move in that direction. We always feel we could be more open, and although it might be difficult to define exactly, it's clear that openness won't be found in a closed mind or some other blinkered state.

Openness is the touchstone of the process of discovery that Rinpoche described. He would go on to say that openness is intrinsic to our being. We don't have to create something we don't have already; we just need to link into the reality of what we are. This is not necessarily easy, but it certainly seems easier to reveal something already within us than to create something from scratch. And it is also easier to practice when we take this point of view.

The instruction to be completely open is an inspiring one. But we do need to know how to apply it in all situations. Trungpa Rinpoche's teaching—and indeed the Buddha's teaching—is about how to bring openness into every experience, and not just meditation. It can easily feel like meditation is here, daily life is over there, and "ne'er the twain shall meet." But they should, and we can learn to practice in such a way as to make this happen.

The simple instruction of openness can be carried into every type of experience: meditation, daily life, and even states of sleeping and dreaming, when awareness may seem to be absent. Trungpa Rinpoche said that if we can develop the quality of awareness during the day, when the mind is idly wandering, it won't be difficult to remain aware during sleep or dreams. We spend many waking hours dreaming, in any case. Waking and dreaming aren't all that different; we just think they are!

Alone, yet Friendly

As you begin to practice, it will become obvious that meditation is both alone and friendly at the same time. By "alone" I mean the experience is yours, and yours alone. Even when you think about the quality of someone else's experience, it is always in terms of your own. There is no other way it could be.

Meditation is also very friendly. It is friendly because all the practitioners of the past have been here before. You are following in their footsteps, and if you experience something genuine—as you will if you persist in it sufficiently—the practitioners of the future will be following in yours.

The Single Thread

Meditation technique is often viewed as something to be kept secret. However there is nothing secret about the basic Buddhist meditation practice I am about to describe. Perhaps I should qualify that. It is what Trungpa Rinpoche called "self-secret." There is no problem in openly explaining the technique, because what you get from it depends entirely on you. There is endless mileage in the practice, in terms of seeing raw data and significance. But only you can experience that; no one can do it for you.

The meditation described here is commonly referred to as *formless meditation*. We could call this a beginners' practice, but it is only for beginners in the sense that we start with it. In fact this is a practice we never abandon. When we reach the highest level—which might have a high-flown name like the Great Perfection—we will find ourselves doing the same meditation.

Formless meditation is associated with the openness and clarity aspects of mind. Within this openness and clarity, gaps occur that make it difficult to remain ego-centered. Egocentricity makes us fearful and shrinking or aggressive and pushy. Either way we're unable to be open, and our clarity is diminished. It is only by joining clarity and openness together that we can act in the world in a precise and genuine way.

Formless meditation is the single thread running through all Buddhist practice. It has great depth and acts as a maturing process for the individual practitioner. Many other practices described are simply ways to work with particular experiences that are difficult to understand or relate to. Such practices may help us to realize what issues there are to work with at all. But all these other seemingly diverse and fascinating techniques arise from this one fundamental method.

3. Body, Speech, and Mind in Meditation

THE MEDITATION TECHNIQUE consists of three parts. The first part relates to the body. The second part relates to speech, which in this case refers to the breath. The breath is the medium for the voice; it is a means of communicating with the outside world and is connected in general with the principle of communication. The third part of the meditation technique relates to the mind, which includes all our thoughts, emotions, and feelings.

Meditation Posture

Meditation is customarily done seated cross-legged on a cushion on the floor. Traditional Buddhists in the East sit in the *vajra* posture—more popularly known as the lotus position—with legs interlocked and the soles of the feet pointing upward. This posture is not so easy for most Westerners, and you need not sit like that. It is enough to sit comfortably in a loose cross-legged position on a mat on the floor. This posture, sometimes called the "tailor's posture," can be quite comfortable. It puts you in contact with the ground that you're sitting on and is the best way to sit, unless you have a problem with your back or some other part of your anatomy. The alternative is to sit in a chair. Trungpa Rinpoche taught that it is not the physical posture but the mind that really matters.

Some chairs are more suitable than others for meditation. It is best to use a simple comfortable chair with no arms, like a kitchen chair. Try not to lean against the back, unless you have a serious health problem. Folding your feet under the chair is less stressful than stretching them out. Apart from that, the posture is the same as when sitting on the floor.

The most important instruction with regard to posture is to keep a straight back, but not ramrod straight or overly proud. Just be relaxed, awake, and upright. A slumped posture is the very antithesis of being alert. Symbolically it says, "I am crushed." Some people sit or walk as if the weight of the whole universe were focused on their backs. A hunched posture also prevents us from breathing well, and we easily get sleepy and uncomfortable. So keep the back more or less straight, with the shoulders dropping slightly backward.

You needn't remain completely still during meditation. If your legs begin to feel numb you can move them. This is not a grim, gritted-teeth approach to meditation. You don't have to suffer unnecessarily. But when a feeling of discomfort makes you want to move, first turn your attention to that feeling. Don't immediately react to it. Allow your mind to rest on the feeling that is pushing you to change your posture. Stay with that feeling just a little longer than you normally would, and then move. Often a slight, almost invisible movement is enough.

You will soon discover that much of your physical discomfort is created by the mind. You may be inwardly groaning with discomfort when, suddenly, the mind slips into a meditative flow and your legs are no longer painful and you feel comfortable. It is important to notice such changes when they occur. I will have more to say about this when we come to the mind aspect of the practice.

In the basic meditation posture—sometimes called the posture of "absolute relaxation"—your hands are placed over the knees. In traditional pictures, the fingers may actually touch the ground. A good way to find the right position is first to let your fingers touch the ground. Then slide your hands back over your knees and onto your thighs, until you feel physically relaxed, with a sense of wakefulness and alertness.

Another traditional Buddhist name for this posture is the *double earth-touching mudra*. It expresses the idea of confidently taking your place on

the earth. It comes from the time when the Buddha made his last meditation before becoming enlightened. At that time, he was attacked by negative forces, which could be thought of as external but also as coming
from within his mind. By touching the ground, the Buddha called on the
earth to witness that he had practiced in a genuine way, not just in that
life but also in past lives. So he had every right to sit there, just as we have.
We can sit with the natural, genuine presence of a human being on this
earth.

Many of us can identify with this attack and its message: "You have
no right to sit here! Go away!" But forget about questions of worthiness
and unworthiness. We exist because we have bodies, because we breathe,
because thoughts come into our minds and pass away. We are part of this
earth and there is nothing we can do about it. We are here, wherever
"here" happens to be. So the question of being worthy or unworthy
doesn't arise, and that point is emphasized by the way we sit on the ground
in meditation.

Basic Confidence

As Westerners, many of us have little confidence in our existence in the
world. It's as if we want to apologize for being here, to become like shad-
ows, to fade away so no one notices us. Obviously this varies from person to person, but it's common to have some affinity with this lack of
basic confidence. So when we take the meditation posture, it's important
to think that we have a right to our position in the world. We have a right
to sit here and relax our mind, to experience who and what we are, what
our mind is, and what our body is, in relation to the space around it. These
are very simple things that everyone has and everyone can do.

Seeing the natural simplicity of our physical presence is the first aspect
of Buddhist confidence. It is meaningless to ask "Am I worthy to be here?"
We are here, so that question has no meaning. We don't have to feel proud
about it either. When we sit in meditation posture, we simply connect to
the earth, to the environment, and to our bodies with the natural confidence of being the way we are. The universe has no antagonism toward

us, and no one is creeping up to stab us in the back. The idea is to feel simple confidence in just sitting and just being.

With Open Eyes

In Buddhist meditation, the idea is not to turn inward. We always need some connection to what is going on around us, which is why we don't shut our eyes in this meditation. Closing the eyes suggests, if only symbolically, that we are shutting ourselves off. In the same way, having our hands resting in the lap—another very traditional meditation posture—could be thought of as some kind of barrier in this context. Here our intention is to be completely open. This is expressed by resting both hands on our knees and keeping our eyes open. There is nothing between our body and the world outside.

We are not looking here and there around the room; our gaze is directed downward, about forty-five degrees from the horizontal. Don't worry about whether this angle is exact or the eyes are too open or too narrow. Just relax, with your eyes slightly open and without tension. Trungpa Rinpoche taught that we need to be careful not to fixate through the eyes or begin to stare. Staring causes the visual image to become fixed and creates strange flashing colors and residual images. If this happens, just shut your eyes for a moment to stop the pattern and then open them again. It's like thinking about a problem. We don't have to shut our eyes when we do this, but we don't stare fixedly either.

How should we think about the place where we meditate? Most of us don't have space for a dedicated shrine room. We may meditate in a very ordinary place: in our family house, in a familiar room with the children's toys scattered around. Wherever we sit, is important to have a feeling of spaciousness beyond those four walls.

This feeling of spaciousness is, in fact, limitless. If you were outside, you would be aware of the sky, distant hills, and buildings. Flash on this sense of not being confined by the four walls of the room, a sense of natural spaciousness that has no obvious stopping place. Without getting too elaborate, just be aware that you are sitting in space and that this space is your natural home. If you went to the ends of the earth, the space would be the same; if you were put into a tiny cubicle, the space would be the same.

Sit with confidence in your relationship with that space. Recognize the openness and spaciousness all around you, and contribute to that openness by putting your hands on your knees rather than folded in front. It feels good to just sit upright in the space, with a sense of delight in the openness. You feel happy just to sit there, and you can feel confident about yourself and your connection to the space. It is tremendously helpful to have this as your starting point.

At this level of practice, we are more concerned with noticing what is happening than with changing it. The most important thing is to be aware of whatever arises as you practice, but if your legs go to sleep, you need to move them. There are ways to wake them up that involve quite minimal movements. If you allow your legs to become completely numb, it will be difficult to stand up at the end of the session, and it may take quite a while to recover. You don't need to go through that. Just move your legs slightly when they begin to go numb. If you need to, cross and uncross them; but try slight movements first.

Using the Breath as a Vehicle

In the speech aspect of this meditation we use the breath as a vehicle. The breath is the medium for the voice and is associated with the principle of communication. In meditation, the speech aspect is based on the quality of openness and the natural connection between our bodies and the world around us.

As you breathe out, rest in the feeling of the breath leaving the body. Just allow the breath to go out naturally, with a sense of spaciousness and giving away, a sense of the breath giving way into space. Other than this, there is no need to concentrate on the breath in any particular way.

Some meditation methods concentrate on the breath in the solar plexus region or at the tip of the nose, but here we are working with a general sense of the breath leaving the body. You are not so much meditating *on* the breath as meditating *with* the breath. We use the breath as a vehicle for the meditation.

On the out-breath, rest the mind on the feeling of the breath leaving the body. Let go into this sensation of space created by the out-breath. As you breathe out into space, don't think that you're filling up space, like a giant balloon. Simply surrender to the feeling of the out-breath leaving the body and the sense of spaciousness that goes with this.

On the in-breath, you can relax by not doing anything at all. Don't follow the breath as it comes in. As Trungpa Rinpoche used to say, it's delightful to know that "you don't have to do anything"; you can "take a holiday" on the in-breath. Just rest where you are. The in-breath is connected with the openness that comes from not having to make things happen.

Then as it goes out again, move with the breath into a greater sense of space. And when that wave of breath ends, relax on the in-breath. With each out-breath, there is a sense of letting go and relaxing farther into space, but without trying to inflate the space or make it bigger. The out-breath is connected with the openness that comes from letting go.

A Sense of Enjoyment

Meditation is not like *Star Trek*: you are not using the spaceship of breath to voyage into infinite space. You are just relating to the sense of space in an ever greater way. You are not pushing at some kind of "space boundary" and you don't need to feel bound by a sense of something beyond the next "breath-horizon." With no boundaries to push back, it's enough just to rest in openness.

So keep the meditation simple, keep it relaxed, and keep your awareness lightly on the out-breath. It's like going with a wave: as each wave finishes, you can rest. There is no sense of having to measure or go farther. Just enjoy yourself.

What makes meditation difficult is thinking that we have too many jobs to do within each cycle of breath. We worry about having to complete the program, or having to cover a certain amount of breath-distance before the next breath comes in. The most important thing is to enjoy riding the breath, with a sense of expansion and relaxation. I don't know anything about surfing, but I suspect it's a good image for this.

We often have such an unforgiving attitude toward ourselves that when we start to enjoy our meditation, we automatically think something is wrong. If the practice seems to be going well, without much ego-centered effort, we may think it's somehow unfair. Well that's the idea! It is probably a good sign to feel that you are cheating. If you are enjoying your practice without seeming to put much into it, you're probably approaching genuine meditation.

Not to harp on this point, but there is a common idea that Buddhism is all about suffering and that being Buddhist means you have to be miserable. Consequently when meditation is enjoyable, something must be wrong; but not so. So please bear this in mind when you meditate: enjoyment is good!

Neither Follow nor Suppress

We would need no further instruction if we could just rest in the openness of the out-breath. But our minds don't work in that way. After a few minutes we get bored with the breath. Thoughts start coming up: "Surely it's time to finish!" "What shall I have for dinner today?" Whole strings of thoughts arise. This is not a problem if we relate to them the right way. Normally, however, we follow these chains of associations. Skipping from here to there and back again, we fill time and space, minute to minute, hour to hour, day to day.

In meditation we neither follow after thoughts and feelings nor try to suppress them. Going beyond either extreme, we just allow them to be. Our minds continually boil with thoughts, and any attempt to suppress them is part of the same process. Trying to stop a thought arising simply replaces it with another kind of thought—the idea of blankness; and any emotional qualities are replaced with another kind of emotion—the emotion of rejection.

Becoming Better Acquainted

In meditation, we acknowledge the thoughts and feelings that arise from moment to moment. We turn toward them, experience them fully, and let them go, again and again, like a good host receiving guests. Of course, you can't spend all your time with one guest; there are plenty more to come. Naturally, a good host doesn't say to one guest, "How wonderful, come straight into the heart of the party!" while saying to another, "I don't like you! Go away!" In meditation, we train to behave equally toward everything that arises in our mind.

When a thought arises, attend to it, feel its flavor and emotional quality, and then let it go. You can then return to the out-breath. A particularly oppressive thought may seem to present itself again and again. Should that happen, don't take the attitude "I've seen you before," because you haven't. What you really mean is "I've seen somebody like you!" It would be ridiculous to say this to a guest or to dismiss someone because you've met the person before. No matter what appears, try to treat each one with equal awareness.

You should also try not to feel bored, even with very familiar thoughts and feelings, but, of course, you will. And so the sense of boredom becomes just another aspect of the party that needs to be felt and addressed. By working in this way, you will gradually find yourself well acquainted with every part of your mind.

Becoming acquainted in this way can be quite difficult sometimes. There is so much going on, and some of it might be quite heavy or negative. We may even feel like killing someone. At first, most of us think of meditation as a kind of holy activity. Consequently we are somewhat guarded with our thinking. But at some point we drop our guard, and then we might get really angry about something.

Given the opportunity just about anything and everything will arise in our minds. And when something really nasty appears, we may not want to admit that we ever think or feel such things. Again, we never turn away from anything, but always turn toward and experience it fully.

Patrul Rinpoche, a great nineteenth-century meditation master, once said that everything that arises in the mind during meditation, no matter what, is sacred. As long as you work with it in the right way, any kind of thought may arise; nothing is excluded. Patrul Rinpoche was part of the Rimé movement in Tibet. *Rimé* means "unbiased." The teachers of this approach trained in unbiased attitudes toward each other and their own minds.

In the context of meditation, bad thoughts aren't treated as bad, good thoughts aren't good. We simply encompass them with awareness, let them go, and return to the out-breath. This is easier said than done of course. We have the inveterate habit of instantly judging thoughts and feelings as good or bad. However, it isn't really a problem when this happens. We simply need to be aware that any judgment is equally just another content of the mind.

Just a Trick of the Mind

At times, there may not be very much going on in your mind. At other times, your mind is in turmoil and you want to be up and away. There might be a very strong emotion behind this that needs to be turned toward and acknowledged. Try not to allow any thoughts and feelings to get behind you and direct the meditation, like a puppet master manipulating a puppet. It's very important to acknowledge all thoughts and feelings as just that, and not give any of them a special status.

In meditation there are generally three things going on. First, there is the object of meditation. Second, there is the person who seems to be meditating. Third, there is the judge or commentator, who constantly takes the meditative temperature, determines whether we are winning or losing, when it's time to finish, and what to do next—the person in charge of events. It's like a seemingly reasonable person standing back and watching the meditation show through binoculars, deciding how well we are doing. But that commentator is not external to the stream of thoughts passing through our minds.

So when a particular set of thoughts or emotions gets behind you, realize it is just a trick of the mind. Everything is part of the practice. And any sense of someone directing events or making reasonable decisions is just another thought or feeling.

The whole basis of Buddhist meditation is to see the contents of our minds as they are, without judging them. This is the first step, but in some sense, it's the whole thing. By doing that we begin to relate to our state of being, not just to the superficiality of our mind. And we don't allow the judgmental mind to send us scurrying off or convince us we're not suited to meditation. In fact, everybody is suited to this kind of meditation because, basically, all our minds are the same. Meditation is about relating to the mind in the simplest, most direct way possible. And while that might be irritating or seem difficult to do, any irritation and difficulty is equally just another part of the mind's display.

Meditation is part of our sanity as human beings. It is a natural function of the mind and, in some sense, a natural function of the body. There are other methods where you try to invent yourself as a better person, but that won't help you see the contents of your mind as they actually are. This meditation is about relating to the mind as simply and directly as we can. And as we sit quietly, experiencing our thoughts and feelings, we can be confident that this is not only something we need or want to do; it is part and parcel of being human.

Meditative Hypochondria

Ambition is such a feature of our culture and the way we are brought up that we can't really avoid it. Ambition is part of the very essence of Western society, although I suspect we could find ambitious meditators everywhere.

When we meditate we look for success in one way or another. In the West, it's very common to think that meditation is about getting rid of thoughts. It's a notion that can be very difficult to shift. As we begin to practice, we worry about getting it right, and we complain when our meditation is full of thoughts, without realizing that those boiling, bubbling thoughts aren't a problem, even if they make us uncomfortable.

Later we wonder if we're getting the results we expected, and we have many ideas about what those results should be. We have notions about attaining enlightenment, although we don't really know what that is. We read about *insight* in the Theravada tradition and *satori* in Zen; or we turn to Tibetan Buddhism and read about *mahamudra* and *dzogchen*. We're always trying to attain something from meditation, something that will make it all worthwhile.

We find ourselves looking over our shoulder during meditation to see how far we've come. We build so many expectations, wishes, hopes, and fears into our practice. But when we meditate to realize something, we've already started down the wrong path—wrong because it turns away from our immediate experience. We compare the past with some imagined future, looking for evidence of improvement.

What's more, we look to other peoples' paths and wonder, "How are they getting on? Am I doing as well as they are, or are they going further and faster along the path?" If we aren't careful, they become rivals or competitors, and our practice turns into a kind of spiritual hypochondria, where we are forever taking our meditative temperature.

What we need to do is really quite simple: to direct our meditation practice toward our immediate experience: toward the breath and the stream of thoughts that arise and pass away. With this attitude, a truly carefree spirit begins to emerge. But this can't happen if we're constantly worrying about our meditative health and attainments, because we will always be looking away from our immediate experience.

Our Real Friend

When we meditate, we may be forever worrying if we're too sleepy or too energetic and wondering whether we should use some trick to settle the mind. We could practice deep breathing, for example, or imagine bright lights. Such tricks may even work for a while; but in the end, they just create more mental disturbance and stop us from focusing on our real friend, simple awareness. In this approach we don't depend on tricks; we rely on the simplicity of awareness.

One big issue for meditators is sleepiness and dullness. If you regularly find yourself becoming sleepy, it might be because of the time you meditate or various other practical considerations. The only instruction that

Trungpa Rinpoche gave me for dealing with sleepiness was to suggest that you could wash your face, and then think briefly of open countryside before you. It's common to be told to do something like this.

You might also try going with the sleepiness, which is something we tend to resist. As you feel yourself nodding off, deliberately relax and go down into that feeling. You may well find yourself rising upward, like a bubble, out of that sleepy state. It's the opposite of our normal response, which is why it sometimes works. It can be good to startle your mind out of its old habits occasionally. By going with the feeling of sleepiness, rather than fighting it, you may find the energy to perk you up.

Alternatively, just think of sleepiness as something that happens to all of us from time to time. It is not so terrible to feel sleepy, and you can treat any judgmental voice that says "this makes you a bad meditator" as just another thought.

Unless there is something fundamentally wrong, our minds will display every kind of state from time to time: dullness, depression, and sleepiness; and their opposites, where the mind energetically boils with thoughts. It is no good thinking you need a bag of tricks to deal with all this. They often don't work very well in any case.

The most important thing is the attitude you have toward your mind and world. In meditation and in everyday life, the unawakened mind will sometimes feel sleepy, dull, depressed, or excited. But we can just treat them all the same.

Should you feel sluggish, you can sluggishly think that your sluggishness is just another thought, just another way the mind works. You might open out to the experience and briefly pop out of that state, only to fall straight back into it again because the dullness is so strong. It doesn't matter. You just need to keep on working with your mind in this way.

Depression

A word about depression might be helpful here. There are different kinds of depression, which arise for various reasons. Depression isn't necessarily a low-energy state. One type of depression is quite energetic, but not in the sense of jumping about and doing things; it's more that energy is absorbed or held back in some way.

On the other hand, as Buddhist practitioners we could have a very strong experience of emptiness or the collapse of the three times. We may then feel we have no reason to go on living, because all our drives and wishes are based on the notion of a solid, graspable world, experienced in terms of past, present, and future. But this sense of loss is not depression in the ordinary sense of the word and can be worked through as part of our practice.

Some kinds of depression are an affliction of what Tibetans call the *so-lung,* or life-force energy. If this disturbance grows strong enough, it can put us in physical danger, because the will to live seeps away. Someone suffering from this kind of depression might be told to make a few hundred prostrations or many circumambulations of a stupa to help get their energy going. I know it sounds very strange, but physical force has sometimes been used as a cure in Tibet. Someone might come along and beat you up a little. Of course this has to be done properly to be effective!

Almost anything can be used to take the mind off depression, but physical means are generally easier to work with than more subtle Dharma practices. Once we get some energy going, we might then be able to meditate again. However, if the depression is directly related to Dharma practice, these physical methods may not work. More subtle methods are required because the practitioner is suffering from a kind of subtlety, so the problem has to be addressed at that level.

A Slow-Moving Beast

When we meditate it's easy for things to become rather fraught because we feel that any problems must be cured on the spot. But the mind is not like that; the mind is a slow-moving kind of beast that changes gradually over time. So think of meditation as part of your life, something you will never give up. Your mind will be with you forever, and you don't have to get everything right in the one session.

Formless meditation is taught at the beginning because almost everyone can relate to it to some degree. Everyone has a body, breath, an appreciation of space, and a mind with all its thoughts and judgments, and some clarity of awareness. Everyone possesses these qualities and can relate to them from the start.

At some future point, spaciousness will present itself more strongly; clarity will displace egocentricity; and the movement of energy within space, as it goes out and returns to you, will become the vehicle for helping others in various ways. But the basic set-up will be similar to what you have now. In this sense, you won't have gone anywhere. Obviously, there will have been enormous changes. Nevertheless, your mind, and the natural pattern and structure of your being, will always be with you.

So don't worry if your mind sometimes feels depressed, sleepy, or over-energetic. Your mind will gradually become more stable as you practice and increasingly alive at the same time.

Many Western meditators have a problem with energy. Generally speaking we have too much energy and a fear of being dull or sleepy. For Tibetan practitioners, it's the other way around. While we think we should always be up and doing something with our minds in meditation, they tend to feel it is okay to be lazy. What Tibetans have is the basic confidence that everything is working well, regardless.

Again, the great Patrul Rinpoche said that everything that happens in a meditative situation is, by nature, divine or good. From the traditional point of view, the natural support, or *adhisthana,* that comes from the very being-ness of things will carry you along. If you enter the sphere of meditation as wholeheartedly as you can, it doesn't matter if you feel dull, sleepy, or over-energetic. This *adhisthana* will carry you along for many thousands of years. So you certainly don't have to worry about what happens during one meditation session.

The disadvantage of this approach is thinking that, since everything in the garden is wonderful, we can sit back and doze off. Westerners tend to go to the other extreme and feel that it's all in the moment. There are no millions of future lives or even future meditation sessions; it all has to be solved here and now, which makes us quite frenetic.

In working with openness, it is good to have something of the Tibetan attitude. This allows us to connect with the vastness of the Mahayana view: the vastness of time and space, and the vastness of the qualities within us. With the Mahayana view, we won't worry about sleepiness or laziness. We will have the best of both worlds. Until then, you don't need to worry about feeling dull, sleepy, or disturbed when you practice. Just take it in your stride as a part of meditation and don't let it bother you.

Patterns of Mind

Always try to have a relaxed attitude in meditation, even when your mind is full of the confusion of speediness or dullness. It doesn't matter if you are distracted, spaced out, or inattentive. What matters is to have an accepting attitude toward everything that happens in your mind. If you are spaced out or inattentive, for example, just acknowledge this when your awareness returns, and proceed with the meditation technique. There is no need for violent action to correct what are, after all, just the patterns of your mind.

Later, these patterns will become more inspiring from the Dharma point of view, and we can feel much happier about them. When the mind is speedy, our awareness will also become very precise and effortless at the same time. On the other hand, when the mind is spaced-out, inattentive, or over-relaxed, it can become genuinely clear and spacious. This happens spontaneously, not because of anything we do.

We need to recognize the similarities between the pattern of distraction and precision, and confusion and spaciousness. The same principle of focusing and letting go underlies both. The mind works continually in terms of focusing and letting go. This happens from moment to moment, but also over longer periods of time, and we notice this particularly in meditation practice. It's not a mistake to become aware of these patterns. Our minds may be very dull or they may be very clear when we notice them, but it doesn't matter which. Noticing these patterns is part of the meditation.

By meditating in this way the mind becomes lighter, the sense of oppression lifts, and we become almost carefree. This can be heady stuff! We begin to realize what vistas there are in the mind and what is actually possible. Relating to the mind in this way is much more wholesome and profound than merely calming the mind. Calming the mind could be just another drug and the very opposite of what we need.

4. *Boring, Boring, Boring!*

I NITIALLY, we feel uplifted in our meditation by the mere fact that it's new and holds out some promise. Once we settle into the practice, however, we become bored. And as we deal with the stream of thoughts, feelings, and emotions that arise, a sense of irritation may develop. We grumble internally that we started meditating to become free of thoughts, and now we have more than ever before. In fact it only *seems* like there are more thoughts because we've allowed ourselves the space to notice them. It can be quite a sobering experience to realize just how many thoughts pass through our minds.

Hot Boredom

Once the lid is taken off, all kinds of bubbles boil up in the soup of our mind. We then experience what Trungpa Rinpoche called "hot boredom." Meditation, he once said, is "boring, boring, boring!" This is not what we want to hear. That said, he did have more than one definition of boredom.

Hot boredom is a feeling of tremendous irritation in meditation. We just want to get up and do something else. We feel annoyed with ourselves, with our instructor, with the meditation itself. And we wonder, "Why am I doing this when I could be enjoying myself?" Or more subtly, "Why am I meditating when I could be doing something more useful for others?"

These feelings of sharpness, heat, irritation, and annoyance often come from a sense of ambition: "This isn't what I asked for! I didn't join the army of meditators to be bored out of my mind! I really thought I'd get somewhere and it isn't happening! I want to be up and away!" This is a crucial point, because we could be up and away. But if we abandon the practice, we'll never get beyond our ambition.

This is another example of the reasonable person making judgments about our meditation: "It's not working, is it?" We need to realize this is just the mind up to its tricks again. The irritation, no matter how strong and compelling it seems, is simply another feeling that we have to turn toward in an open fashion.

If we get sucked into hot boredom in the wrong way, it can drive us to abandon the meditation altogether. Maybe we should try out Sufism—and I am saying nothing against Sufism—or some other path? To relate to hot boredom properly, we have to "hang in there." If we have to do this with gritted teeth, then teeth gritting becomes part of the meditation. How long does this hot boredom last? It all depends on you and your past connection with meditation.

At some point the mind gives in. We stop fighting that hot boredom and irritability, all of which seems much worse than it actually is. Of course, we can only know this in retrospect. At the time, our mind boils and our body boils as well. Sitting still is painful. We move about in our seat, but moving is just as painful. Changing posture never seems to work; we feel irritable whatever posture we adopt. Our breath is uneven, our mind is unhappy, our emotions are prickly, and we can't sit still. We seem totally unsuited to this meditation.

At this point we just need to give in. There is no technique for doing this. We give in by giving in. We allow ourselves to go though all that irritability and come out the other side. This could be called creative despair. With ordinary despair we just get depressed. Creative despair allows us to give up hot boredom. It's as if the mind couldn't be bothered being irritated any more.

Cool Boredom

At that point, we get the beginning of what Trungpa Rinpoche called "cool boredom," which is not really boredom as we usually think of it. With cool boredom we become truly carefree. Although the content of hot and cool boredom is the same, suddenly—maybe for the first time—we enjoy being what we are.

Unbelievably, the instant we hit cool boredom, our body suddenly feels fine. Both mind and breath flow more easily. All our bodily discomfort disappears, and we realize it was all a figment of our irritability. It's as magical as that. As our mind and breath settle in this way, the happier part of meditation begins.

My only hesitation in telling you this now is the fear that, in the throes of hot boredom, you will start wondering when the cool boredom is coming; and the fact that it hasn't arrived yet makes for even more irritation. Perhaps there is nothing to be done about that. At least it gives you the confidence that you will eventually come through it. Meditators often feel like giving up when they get their first experiences of hot boredom. But if we want to get the fruit of the practice we have to stay with it. There is nothing else we can do.

Eventually the mind begins to relax spontaneously. We can then consider the continual arising and disappearing of thoughts—and even their flickering, irritating nature—as part of the natural creativity of the mind. We don't have to keep track of them for fear they might undermine or destroy us. We can begin to appreciate the power of our mind and its tremendous energy. We could admire this even though we have no control over it.

It feels almost natural to think that meditation must be about something more than just the ordinary mind. We always want to discipline the mind in some way or another. But trying to use force never works. The mind always resists, and it seems a more gentle approach is much more effective. As the mind relaxes, and the heat of hot boredom begins to dissipate, the stream of thoughts continues just the same. The difference is that we stop caring about their presence—or absence.

This is the beginning of formless meditation, proper. At last we can enjoy the flow of our mind as cool boredom. We have a genuine sense of equanimity, no matter what arises from the continuity of our experience. The mind is light, pleasant, and somewhat carefree, and we feel no need to look for an occupation.

As the mind stops chasing itself, being with ourselves stops being such an irritating experience; it becomes more like a pleasant stream. We feel happy just sitting in meditation, not in a cow-like fashion, but with a genuine sense of stability. We aren't thrown by anything that comes up. Trungpa Rinpoche used to say that when you reached the furthest extent of this quality, you wouldn't be disturbed even if a pterodactyl fell in your lap!

A Healthy Feeling

It can be helpful to say something about the fruits of meditation practice from time to time. Trungpa Rinpoche originally taught me never to hold out any hope to anyone, about anything. He later modified that approach. If we look for results as we practice then we effectively stop meditating, or do so in fits and starts, always testing the meditative temperature. "How am I doing? Has my fever gone down yet? Am I anywhere near cool boredom?"

The advantage of holding out no hope whatsoever is that we learn to meditate without looking for results. Those results can then come spontaneously. There are definite results that come through practice, but we should never look for them.

Going beyond thoughts of worthiness or unworthiness, we eventually find ourselves in the state of cool boredom, where we feel awake and carefree. This isn't some kind of ecstasy. It is more like what Trungpa Rinpoche called "newly-baked bread." It has a healthy feeling about it, but it's enough, and we can rest in this state.

At this point our meditation is moving toward some quality of just being. We may not have arrived yet, but we're on course, and that's all we need worry about. This is the best way to think about the whole of our Dharma practice really. It's certainly better than attempting some ambitious schedule, which only disturbs the heart and mind and makes us sick.

5. A Gently Arising Magic

I T IS QUITE possible to have a genuine experience, connected with awakening, but still miss its significance. It arises suddenly, feels very inspiring and then vanishes. It may have felt significant, but strange to say we're not quite sure what it was. In some ways it's like the tip of an iceberg, which may seem a bit of a cold image. However, the tip tells us there is so much more to discover.

When we first begin to practice, our discoveries might seem somewhat intellectual. But the sense of discovery deepens as we go on. Eventually we get a flash of something that opens us up, something that causes an emotional reaction and really tells us something about the world.

But what can we say about such an experience? People sometimes ask meditators what they get out of meditation. And it may seem very unsatisfactory not to get an answer. But the reason meditators may not be able to answer is that they genuinely can't say. Either they're beginning to touch on something that is truly beyond words; or they've only experienced the tip of something significant. They know from past experience it has meaning, even if they don't know what it is.

When that meaning becomes clearer, they end up using the same language meditators have used for centuries. And so they won't seem to be saying anything new. For instance, you might truly experience the emotional impact of impermanence. The questioner may well respond that there is nothing very interesting in that. But it could be tremendously significant for you as the experiencer; it could change your whole outlook on life. By realizing the evanescence of health and beauty you might become much less obsessed with them.

Or you could understand something about the significance of death. Maybe death will seem less of a big deal. Ordinarily death is a big issue because we don't want to die. It's like going to the dentist, but much more so. The whole of me is going to be removed, not just a tooth! But through seeing something of the significance of impermanence, our take on death and other basic experiences could change. We could become more care-free about death, or realize that death is even more significant, but in ways we never realized before.

Ordinary Magic

One of the earliest instructions Trungpa Rinpoche ever gave to me was, "Don't meditate like a cat watching a mouse hole." The "mice" are our thoughts and feelings, and it's like we sit waiting to pounce on them as they appear. We could be a lot gentler with the whole process.

There is a powerful yet gentle magic about the fact that thoughts arise at all. Ordinary things are totally magical, but it takes a while to see that. Things don't seem magical when we are used to them. We are so accustomed to thoughts and emotions arising in our minds that they don't seem at all mysterious. It's common to think we need to enter into some elaborate psychotherapy to relate to our emotions properly. But the fact that thoughts and feelings appear at all—and what they are in themselves—is amazing.

Rather than investigating why we experience certain thoughts and feelings—and I'm not saying there's no place for that—we could be much more direct. We could ask ourselves, "What are emotions? What are thoughts?" The question "Where do thoughts come from?" is profound, because we can actually find out. The answer is laid out before us. But it's only when we understand that the question has meaning, and has an answer at the level of "seeing significance," that we first begin to realize the magic of ordinary experience.

Could Do Better?

Ambition can be quite subtle, and at this point, we could look at it further. In meditation, we train to let go of ambition; to see that whatever arises in meditation is sufficient in itself, so we need never look beyond our direct experience.

It would be wonderful to meditate like this and, of course, it's encouraged. But none of us does it perfectly. Some sense of ambition is always present, even when we are talking about openness. We feel we're more open at some times than others, and we would like to foster that openness. It seems a genuine thing to do, and our teachers encourage us in this direction. So we still have the idea of a yardstick we can measure ourselves against. And we always feel, as it used to say at the bottom of school reports, "He could do better."

A certain amount of measuring and assessing how we are doing is inevitable. We have to start from where we are. We can't wave a magic wand and make all our problems suddenly vanish. But as long as we say I could be more like this or have less of that, there is some limitation.

The need for yardsticks and measuring rods is much more prevalent and lies deeper within us than we imagine. Merely to realize the strength of our ambition is a kind of revelation. Ambition is part of the baggage we carry around with us, and it could take years to recognize just how pervasive it is.

White Crows and Other Experiences

It is possible to have many and varied meditation experiences that, while they capture our attention, are not actually significant. Such out-of-the-ordinary experiences are just more raw data. If an experience seems to take me to another world, it doesn't necessarily mean that I see any significance in that. I may just end up writing a book about my wonderful, out-of-body experiences.

If you asked Trungpa Rinpoche about things like out-of-body experiences, he would look at you in a bored kind of way. He seemed to view such things as astral projection or near-death experiences as fundamentally boring, because we don't get to see any significance in them. From his point of view, such experiences were just another part of conditioned existence, and not all that interesting. I have known him to be quite dismissive, if not exactly scathing, of such things.

For Trungpa Rinpoche, the most important thing was to see the significance of something. The danger lay in making a big deal of these experiences. That is what makes them problematic. There is a Tibetan saying about white crows. It is very unusual to see a white crow, so people make a big deal out of seeing one. As far as Rinpoche was concerned, these experiences are like white crows.

In the Buddhist context, there is nothing remarkable in such meditation experiences. The only thing that matters is seeing the significance of experience. Our tendency, however, is to think there is a "brownie point" in having such an experience. We look back at it and compare it with our friends. If they haven't encountered anything like it, we feel special. And should we have a genuinely significant experience, then that's an even bigger brownie point. But this is by no means the end of the story.

Over time we may have many experiences of minor significance, along with some extraordinary experiences, both significant and otherwise. Some of these might be genuinely valuable and may even change us in some way. But eventually we realize our accumulated experiences are of no account whatsoever, because they are all rooted in ambition. It was ambition that caused us to practice in such a way as to have these experiences, even the insightful ones.

At the moment we see this clearly, there is the possibility that our ambition could collapse. And when it collapses, everything built on ambition collapses as well. All our experiences, both ordinary and extraordinary, seem just so much nonsense. It is the same old game we've been playing in other areas of our lives: the game of collecting, of making things happen, and trying to manipulate the world in one way or another.

The essential heart of the practice is beyond ambition and manipulation. But we can't will ourselves into that position. We can't work at being unambitious. That is just another kind of ambition, another ego trap. We have to experience the deadliness of ambition and everything that comes from it. We need to press on with the practice, keeping awakened-ness strongly to the fore, until eventually our ambition collapses.

Vomiting Up Ambition

This process of collapse is rather dramatically described as vomiting; we vomit up that whole ambitious way of being. Ambition and confusion are very much tied together. Awareness and openness are the qualities that enable us to pass beyond the deadliness of ambition, so that we just allow things to be. But we resist this strongly. It is as though we've taken the drug of confusion.

We are drugged on unawareness, and this prevents us from vomiting up our confusion, ambition, and everything that goes with it. We simply need to stop taking the drug. This is easier said than done, of course, but it happens eventually. And we don't have to metaphorically put fingers down our throats. The vomiting happens spontaneously, and our ambition comes up and vanishes, like it had never been.

The idea that we might go beyond ambition raises some interesting questions. How could we accomplish anything? How could we do any good in the world? How could we practice meditation without some notion of getting somewhere? The answer is that our volition and creativity don't stop when we vomit up our ambition. They just come from a different place; one uncontaminated by ambition. The only way to reach that place is by applying ourselves to the practice.

The Magic of Persistence

So how does the Buddha's Dharma lead us to see genuine significance? We apply the meditation technique, and eventually we get to some deep insight. But how do we actually get there? Funnily enough, it's not even that much hard work. It is simply the combination of persistence and being as open as we can.

The great yogin Milarepa gave many initiations, instructions, and ways of producing insight to one of his closest students. When this pupil was leaving, Milarepa said, "I want to give you my final instruction, the final teaching, which is the most important of all." Milarepa then lifted his robe and showed his bottom, which was covered in corns and calluses, saying, "This is because I have sat and meditated for such a long time!"

What we need is the energy of persistence. We have nice soft seats, so it probably won't be quite the same for us. But we will need to persist in the same way. The magic of Dharma is just persistence.

Come and See

"Come and see!" This is how the Buddha described his world of openness and awareness. It's wonderful to find such an instruction at the heart of a religion. Religions don't generally promulgate such openness. We might expect, instead, to hear that we need faith in something we don't yet understand. Faith has an important place in Buddhadharma, but its more about having confidence in the truthfulness of the insights that arise as we practice. We can't begin with faith in something we haven't experienced. What we need is the "faith of persistence" as it's sometimes called.

Here, like anywhere else, we need to put our minds to the practice and persist. It's no good learning all these techniques for becoming open and aware if we don't use them. If we lack the confidence or vigor to apply what we know, it will be of no help. This is true in every walk of life, in plumbing or gardening as much as in Buddhism. The path is not an easy, theoretical, or once-a-week adventure. The toughness arises from the fact that we have to be at it all the time. This may sound daunting, and maybe that is good. But it may also sound claustrophobic, which it isn't.

Five Supports

There are ways of working with openness and awareness without it becoming problematic. If someone were always badgering us to be open, it would feel very itchy and claustrophobic, and we would probably walk away. Instead we can learn to relax into the natural rhythm of openness and focusing. Buddhists like lists, and there is a list of five things that are relevant here.

First, we need *vigor and persistence*. We cannot hope to develop insight, understanding, and openness without vigor and persistence.

Second, we need to learn how to *relax* within that.

Third, we need the heart and *confidence* to do it. We can't persist without a reason. We must truly feel there is something of value in this.

Fourth, our understanding of *openness* needs to develop gradually. By learning to be what Trungpa Rinpoche described as "gentle to ourselves and merciful toward others," we are able to apply the path to ourselves, to others, and to the world.

Fifth, we need to understand that *awareness* naturally ebbs and flows; and that there are ways to encourage that awareness within ourselves.

Natural Sensitivity

Most of us wonder if there's a critical mass of realization and practice, after which there is no falling back; and whether we mere mortals can ever expect to reach this point.

There is a stage of practice described as the "nonreversing" stage. It's a bit like pushing something very heavy up a steep hill. This is very hard work until you reach the top, after which you can roll down the other side in an easy fashion.

This doesn't mean that suddenly everything in the garden is lovely. We still go through painful experiences. They may be even more painful, because we can no longer fall back on our capacity to ignore those things we don't like. At the nonreversing stage the veils to our vision have dropped enough for us to see the painful, abrasive nature of experience more clearly. And even pleasurable things can seem painful and sharp if we don't link into them completely. This is all linked to the Buddha's truth of *duhkha*, or suffering.

However, once we enter into things in a completely open way, that painful quality becomes more like an experience of bliss. Actually, it is neither pleasant nor painful, but neither is it neutral. That's why *sensitivity* is such a good word for this. Sensitivity is the opposite of indifference and implies both pain and pleasure. The power of openness and awareness leads to a panoramic vision that removes any sense of claustrophobia in our pain or pleasure.

Openness, awareness, and sensitivity to our internal and external worlds are natural. They are forced on us, whether we like it or not. Without that intrinsic quality of clarity and awareness, how could we be aware of anything around us?

A certain amount of openness is always present, just because the world around us is *other*. However much we try to acquire, manipulate, or conquer that quality of space we are never totally successful. We might resent that openness, and want to push it away, but we can't deny its existence.

Our natural sensitivity is connected to the emotions, and the way we feel about the world. It might express itself as "I don't want this!" or "I wish I weren't here!" People who commit suicide sometimes do so as an expression of sensitivity—a wish for that sensitivity to cease. But openness, awareness, and sensitivity are given. Without them we wouldn't exist. They are always present and we have to learn to work with them.

Revolutionary Simplicity

In Buddhist practice, we often stress the importance of openness, awareness, and sensitivity. Through this simple approach we learn about our worlds, and at first we may not realize just how revolutionary it is.

We could use openness, awareness, and sensitivity as techniques. But the technique basically consists of an attitude: you are the king or queen of your world, and everything is placed before you; nothing is left out. There is a wonderful simplicity in this. You don't need extra tools, techniques, or some special wisdom from elsewhere. Wisdom lies within your being in a very direct and simple way. The only difficulty is in connecting with that simplicity. All the techniques, advice, and occasional sticks and carrots are skillful means: gradual ways to help us realize it is all here and now, to be discovered directly in our own nature.

A Siren Call

Our nature, our being, is not connected with egocentricity or selfishness. There is no separate, concrete self within our being or experience. Belief in such a self, or the notion that it is necessary, is part of the enchantment, a siren call: "Without me you couldn't think, see, smell, taste, or emote; you couldn't feel good or bad." And this, it turns out, is complete rubbish. Our very ego-centeredness is what gets in the way of our thinking, feeling, experiencing, and relating to things properly. Even in the conventional sense, we say, "My ego got in the way."

The Buddha's Dharma can sound like a great campaign against ego, but it's hard to get rid of something that never existed in the first place. From the Buddhist point of view, ego is just a wrong idea that we need to let go of.

Through the practice of meditation, we gradually realize that our mind is indeed obstructed. We want to be open, clear, and happy, and be able to relate to others, but something seems to get in the way. Once we experience this directly, we can no longer take such a rosy view of the universe. But interestingly, it is also possible to paint too gloomy a picture.

I once knew a woman who could never get very far with her practice. She got started easily enough. But then she would resort to the language of therapy and say things like: "How can I trust my experience? It always lets me down. There's always a problem. Whenever I do something, I feel I'm doing it for reasons I'm unaware of." Thinking like this is fundamentally stultifying. If we don't trust our experience, we can make no steps toward understanding. And when insight does arise, we won't be sure we experienced it.

East and West

A genuine insight could be so strong, clear, and unmistakable that it becomes the touchstone of our existence from that point onward. However, it rarely works like that. Most insights are incomplete and don't go that far. So how are we to judge such an experience?

I once asked a Tibetan friend about this. He said there were three possibilities: it could be genuine understanding, it could be possession by a demon—which is the Tibetan context coming through—or the person could be going mad! In the West we would probably discount the second option, so we are left with the choice between genuine insight or madness.

Why might we think we were going crazy? Well, we only need to experience things differently to understand this. A genuine experience of the nature of your world may be unexpected and mind-blowing; certainly not the kind of thing talked about on the radio or in newspapers, or even in therapy. If we have tremendous confidence we can ignore the totality of our peers and say, "They just don't understand!" But then, that is just the kind of thing mad people say...

This seems to be less of an issue in the East. If you had such an experience there, probably no one would wave a flag or make a fuss, but those around you would most likely consider it a good thing. An uncle or some other close relative may well have encountered something similar, and there would be local teachers who could guide you further. That's how it works in a traditional culture, where it's all taken for granted.

Eastern Buddhists are equally alive to the possibility of madness. But in the West, we tend to ignore the validity of insight, except perhaps in the circumscribed area of psychotherapy. For that reason, it's important to become part of a practicing Buddhist community. Then you have the wider tradition and community around you, and hopefully they will be supportive when you have such experiences, or when such experiences begin to change you. It would be assumed that any such changes would be to the good.

A Feeling for Truth

How can we know we are genuinely relating to direct experience rather than just fooling ourselves? The only way to tell is by feeling the general direction of your practice. If egocentricity and attachment seem to be increasing as you practice, you're probably following the wrong path. On

the other hand, if your mind is becoming more naked, clear, and open—
all of which are relative—you are probably on the right path.

It's your mind, and only you can know whether it's genuine openness
or mere confusion. You can get advice from your teachers about this. That
is indispensable, as is the companionship of those who tread the path with
you. Teachers and fellow practitioners can genuinely help you sharpen
your awareness and connection with Dharma. But in the end it always
comes down to you. That is the meaning of direct experience.

People sometimes ask how they can tell if their meditation practice is
working. There are three answers to that, and they all have some truth to
them. The first answer is that we'll never know if our meditation is successful, except in the very long term. So why bother asking?

The second, more common answer, tells us that with confidence, all
meditation is successful. Whether we feel good or bad about it, we are
training in the Dharma, and that is good in itself. The most important
thing in meditation, generally speaking, is an attitude of openness. With
that attitude, there is no need to worry about whether our meditation is
good or bad.

The third and more subtle answer is to say that we have a natural faculty that will eventually lead us to the truth. Sometimes we can feel an
inherent rightness—or wrongness—about our meditation. How accurate
is this feeling? While it could be mistaken, it's a basic Buddhist principle
that a faculty of genuineness, a feeling for truth, exists with us. We can't
prove it, but all the evidence over centuries of Buddhist practice suggests
this is the case. As time goes by, our practice deepens and we get more of
a feel for what is right and wrong.

Right from the Start

The general idea in meditation is to be open and clear. Openness and clarity are vague terms, but fortunately just the words alone are enough to
start us off in the right direction. As we go on, they come to have a more
precise and direct meaning. And in the end we can link into clarity and

openness as a direct experience. But those ordinary words provide an invaluable starting point.

Gradually, a kind of intuitive wisdom takes over. Initially this wisdom is shaped by the words themselves, but as it feeds back, the words come to have a much more precise meaning. The general direction was right from the start, but through our practice we come to know much more about the real meaning of openness and clarity.

We rely on this fundamental ability to discriminate in all our Dharma training, not just in meditation. Why is it right to work toward transcending ego? Maybe ego is a really good thing? We find that difficult to believe, and again, we are right about that from the start.

If we have questions about the meaning of existence, there is a realm where such answers can be found. But we will never be able to explain it in conceptual terms, not even to ourselves. What we have is a faculty to experience these answers directly. This faculty steers us through the path of meditation and awakens us to the true nature of things. That faculty could itself be described as truth.

Trungpa Rinpoche once said that the only method the Buddha taught was meditation. By meditation he meant the development of openness, from which clarity and then sensitivity arise. This is all that we have to work with, but it is all we need. We undervalue and undersell ourselves by thinking we need anything more.

There is a wonderful simplicity and directness to this practice. We now need to look at ways of applying it to our everyday lives.

6. Openness and Everyday-Life Practice

SITTING MEDITATION is vital as a basis for everyday-life practice, but it isn't enough. Daily-life practice is important because most of us spend only a small amount of time in formal meditation. However, we do have to be realistic about what is possible.

The daily-life practice, which is traditionally called the *post-meditation experience,* covers everything we do outside of formal sitting meditation. Trungpa Rinpoche used to say that everyday-life practice isn't what most of us think it is. Practitioners often believe that practicing in daily life is about trying to be continuously aware of their bodies, feelings, sense perceptions, and states of mind. There is nothing wrong with this idea; these are the traditional raw materials of practice. The important thing, however, is how we relate to them.

We have to avoid becoming observers of our experience. There is a certain superficial attraction in being an observer. Indeed, this is how awareness practice was sometimes taught by early Western Buddhist teachers. By becoming an observer we can distance ourselves from painful emotions and experiences. We may seem to experience our thoughts, feelings, and emotions very clearly, while remaining separate from them at the same time. But this is like watching the world from behind a glass window; and we will never truly experience its nature by doing that.

For a while, we might appear to be a very calm, controlled sort of person. But it's like we have a tiger by the tail. At some point the emotion gets too strong, and we can't maintain that sense of division any longer. Eventually we may get a big emotional explosion as the sense of separation suddenly collapses. It all bursts out in an uncontrolled way. Or our minds go blank, and we lose all awareness. Why? Because we have been working in terms of control and distance.

It was Trungpa Rinpoche who pricked this particular bubble for me. He said that was not the way to practice awareness. Instead, we need to open out toward the flow of our thoughts and feelings, to the point where there is no distance between ourselves and our emotions.

Should we worry about being taken over when we let go into the emotion and the feeling? We tend to distance ourselves a little most of the time anyway, but that is just ego trying to control things. They say that where there's awareness without that sense of separation, the emotions don't run wild in a stupid or crazy fashion. You will have to try this for yourself to prove that it is true. It is one of the axioms of the path we follow that by opening out to situations with awareness, a spontaneously compassionate response will arise.

The Coin of Tension

To adopt the attitude that "I am here, observing the world out there" is the beginning of a big mistake. At the back of our minds, we think we can control the world through our awareness. And as we attempt to do this, it often happens that awareness does increase. Because we are attending to things more carefully than we normally would, our awareness brightens a little, and we naturally want this to continue. So we cling to this contrived state of awareness.

The mind has a natural rhythm of focusing and letting go. It won't allow us to focus forever. We can focus, focus, focus, and then suddenly the mind will let go. The mind does this by itself, whether we want it to or not. And when this happens, we might start blaming ourselves for not trying harder or holding on longer, which is the beginning of a disaster.

By making a great effort, our awareness may indeed get a little brighter. But the coin we get paid back in is the coin of tension. It's like trying to balance on top of a pyramid. Dr. Johnson's famous words seem appropriate here: "It is not done well, but you are surprised to find it done at all!" Meanwhile we try to control the world by looking out at it through the glass window of contrived mindfulness.

We practice in this way because we think we'll get something out of it. But in the end it becomes so painful we abandon the effort and give up the whole idea of awareness, or choose some other path.

A bit of contrived mindfulness can't be helped; we are still living in the conditioned world; but we can at least try to ameliorate the situation rather than making it worse. Trungpa Rinpoche described contrived mindfulness as a child hiding behind its mother's skirts. The mother is *prajna,* or wisdom. The child peeps out at the world, using wisdom as a kind of defense, which is not its proper basis.

Just Do It!

What is the correct way to relate to our experience mindfully and with awareness? According to Trungpa Rinpoche, the important thing is not to have a *program* of awareness. Try instead to connect with whatever arises very directly; you have to give in to it.

If you find yourself in a difficult situation, don't think, "I am going to be aware of whatever happens around me!" Just allow yourself to experience it simply. Without trying to protect yourself, or feeling the need for tricks or techniques, open out to whatever happens and experience it as directly as you can.

Trungpa Rinpoche taught that it doesn't matter if you don't know what to do when you open out like this. Don't worry about that. If you don't know what to do, let that be the case. Just open—immediately and simply—to your experience and allow it to carry you. His analogy was a cook: a good cook doesn't question whether or not he can cook; he just cooks. And that is how we should be. Just go ahead, without questioning whether or not you can do it. You may not be a perfect cook, but this seems to be the only way to really learn about our experience.

A New Way of Looking at the World

We can apply the practice of openness to all the varied situations of our daily lives. Much of the time we find ourselves in a neutral state, where we are neither disturbed or elated. Under these circumstances it's fairly easy to turn our minds to some specific practice. But when we're in a state of emotional turmoil or difficulty, our problems seem more pressing, and we want to do something about the situation.

In this case, we are instructed not to obey our first reaction, which is to turn away from unpleasant situations. At first you may think, "I don't want to be involved in this," and pretend it's not there. Or you may realize that you're about to be put on the spot in some way. You see it coming, and you dearly wish things were different.

One attitude we can take in such situations is to shrink away and try to avoid them. Alternatively, we become aggressive and want to destroy or attack them. But instead of striking out or avoiding things, we should turn toward the situation, no matter what happens. Open out toward it without defending yourself, with empty hands, like a naked warrior with no weapons or armor. Turn toward the situation by opening yourself out, and allow yourself to experience it before making a response.

Most of us dread bad or uncomfortable situations, wondering what we can do to make them less unpleasant. But as far as the practice is concerned, that isn't the point. Surrendering to a situation might indeed make us feel better, but that is not the purpose of the exercise. Surrendering allows us to feel the qualities of a situation and to see things clearly. If we turn away or respond with aggression, we never get the chance to do that.

So even if you feel that the situation that's about to unfold might be so embarrassing, frightening, or difficult you would never recover from it, just open out to it. It may appear like a high wall that you can't see beyond, but you will pass through it and come out the other side. It's going to happen anyway, and one way or another you will deal with it. So take the attitude "Even if this situation destroys me...." Logically, you know this won't happen. You will live through the experience. But by entering into the situation with openness, you have a chance to see its nature. You get to taste the whole situation, just as you would in formless meditation. You get to treat it as a guest rather than an adversary.

Turning toward the situation creates the opportunity for some kind of genuine response. In the beginning, we may be so astonished that we can do this that nothing much happens. But that feeling is enough. There will be many other situations in our lives where we can apply this method. Sooner or later, we realize that opening out toward things isn't such a big deal. It's just a first step.

We start by feeling the basic ground of the situation. From this comes the inspiration to do something. Who knows what that might be? You might find that it wasn't so terrible after all, and you can respond in a joyful fashion. You might find yourself responding in ways that surprise both you and everyone else. There are many possibilities. With the quality of openness, a kind of lightness creeps into the situation. This is the beginning of a new way of looking at the world.

PART 2. MANDALA PRINCIPLE

& The Cause of Suffering

"O God, I could be bounded in a nutshell,
and count myself a king of infinite space,
were it not that I have bad dreams."
—William Shakespeare, *Hamlet*

*Mandala is a neutral force. Good or bad, awakened
or unawakened, everything in the universe manifests
in terms of mandala principle.*

7. A Universe of Mandalas

M ANDALA is a Sanskrit word that has come into common
use. You come across it in the writings of Carl Jung, for
example. It occurs in Indian religion generally, and in Buddhism it is usually presented in terms of the deities and their palaces depicted in Tibetan
paintings. But mandala, as the term is used here, is a much more general
principle, and every aspect of our experience, both internal and external,
can be understood in terms of mandala.

Like many other aspects of Dharma, mandala is a neutral force. The
presence or absence of awakened vision makes something enlightened or
unenlightened—our actions may be considered good or bad depending
on whether they are narrowly ego-centered or not—but in every case the
way things operate is the same. Good or bad, awakened or unawakened,
everything in the universe manifests in terms of mandala principle.

Basic Principles

Mandalas exist in our minds, in society, and in the physical world around
us. Everything in the universe expresses itself in terms of mandala and
interlocking mandalas within mandalas.

The word *mandala* literally means "round" or "circular," but it is
sometimes glossed as *manda* meaning essential essence, and *la* meaning

the periphery. Mandalas work in terms of center and periphery, or center and emanation. At the center is the basic organizing principle, which is something active and powerful. Symbolically, the basic principle is often represented by a dot.

Emanating from the central principle are various related subprinciples. These form the body of the mandala, which is often depicted as a sphere with a quite definite boundary. The writ and power of the fundamental principle doesn't run beyond the boundary, although its influence may extend further in a weakened form. Whenever mandalas have to do with people and their concerns, the boundary is a very emotional place.

The simplest form of a mandala is a circle with a center and an inside and outside. Because this is merely symbolic it conveys neither the emotional cohesiveness that makes up the interior nor the emotional significance of the boundary, but it's a serviceable image. The sun and moon are sometimes described as mandalas in this sense.

Around the boundary are the mandala guardians. The guardians keep the internal elements within the mandala boundary and prevent outside elements from breaking in. If certain elements within the mandala become rebellious, surplus, or unsuitable, they are thrown out, while new elements may be absorbed from outside.

Another key aspect of mandala principle is the energy exchange between the different elements of the mandala, and between the inside and outside. A living mandala is something dynamic, not a piece of fixed geometry, and it is that life-energy exchange that holds it all together. That energy flows along connections called *samayas*.

Samaya is a Sanskrit word that means bond or connection. It is a term found in Buddhist tantra but has more general application as part of mandala principle. I have a bond with my parents whether I like being in their mandala or not. It's a fact of my existence. Likewise, I have a strong bond with the language I was brought up with. I see the world in a certain way because of the language I speak, and in turn, I influence that language, if only in a very small way.

These connections can be represented by the radial and transverse spokes of a bicycle wheel. A spider's web is another good image for this, provided you can think of it without the less happy associations.

Mandalas Are Everywhere

Probably the easiest way to understand mandala principle is by looking at specific examples, both within our minds and in the world outside.

We can see mandala principle operating around us all the time. Physical things like houses, cars, and planes are mandalas. Streets, neighborhoods, cities, and countries form mandalas within mandalas.

Even a simple container like a cup forms a very crude mandala: its main principle is to contain liquid, the liquid it contains makes up the body of the mandala, and the boundary is the cup itself. The emotional aspect of the boundary is whether the cup leaks; we certainly feel very unhappy when tea spills in our laps!

People in an audience form a mandala just by being in the same room. Individuals working together on a project create a more integrated mandala. The students around a teacher form a mandala, as do workers in a department within a larger organizational mandala.

Social Mandalas

A political party is a complex social mandala. Its central principle may be to change society in a particular direction or, more narrowly, to get its leaders elected to positions of power. Within the mandala is the body of those who subscribe to its principles. Outside the boundary are those who think and vote differently.

One of the functions of a political party is to win over at least some of those outsiders. Anyone wishing to pass through the boundary and enter the mandala must be in harmony with its basic principles. Any elements that are in conflict with them are thrown out. The boundary is like a filter or a living organism, and anything disharmonious is ejected. So we see things from outside being absorbed inward, foreign elements that have crept inside being thrown out, and other elements hovering around the boundary.

Emotions are very strong on the boundary, especially when there is any uncertainty. In this example there may be people who can't decide whether they belong in the party or not. There is a kind of paranoia about this. Are they traitors? Or would they like to be? Should they be allowed in? We often get very emotional about people and things we can't classify, and there is generally a strong sense of problem about this kind of boundary.

A nuclear family is a mandala. Whether we are father, mother, child, or adopted into the family, the central principle has to do with emotional closeness. We might struggle to put a finger on the essence of that closeness, but it draws the family members together and creates a mandala. Again, the boundary is a very emotive one. In a divorce one parent may be planning to leave but remains apparently inside the mandala, and this is tremendously emotive, especially for the children.

In a family mandala, energy flows from the parents to keep the family together and to support the children as they grow up. And something comes back from the children to the parents. Parents commonly feel that their lives are in their children in some way. It's the interplay of this life energy that holds the mandala together.

A Dynamic Process

The English language is another kind of mandala. There is a central ethos of Englishness, and then the specific elements that make up the internal structure of the language: the words, spelling, grammar, punctuation, and so on. The boundary has to do with correctness. Is it proper English? What about American or Australian English? We get very worked up about notions of correct versus incorrect English, and this is true of any language. It may be fuzzy, but there is always a boundary of some kind, and a decision to be made about whether a word or expression falls inside or outside it.

The exchange of energy between the center and periphery is a dynamic process. The English language is not just a set of fixed rules. The conventions of correct English influence those who speak the language. But those who speak English eventually feed back into and influence the language itself, so we can't really separate the two.

Codes of behavior also change over time, in much the same way. Those of a hundred years ago vary in many respects from those we follow now but aren't completely different. And again, we get emotional about people on the boundary. Are they "our" sort of person? Does their actual behavior conflict with the way they present themselves? We feel happy with those firmly inside our social mandala and comfortable enough with others who are clearly outside. The problem lies with those who sit on the fence, which is always an uncomfortable place to be.

The Mandala of You and Your World

The most obvious example of a mandala is you in your world. You are in the center of your world. Everything that appertains to you is the energy, or power, of that mandala. All your belongings and attachments make up the central body of the mandala. Outside the boundaries of your mandala are the external things over which you have no control or that you want nothing to do with. The boundary is the emotional area made up of all the decisions and dilemmas around what is or isn't yours.

This may seem a silly image, but people do make a lot of fuss about garden fences. Whose fence is it? Is it on my side or your side of the fence? Quite ridiculous and extreme conflicts can arise over such issues. A tree grows in my garden, but the fruit falls in yours, and this causes a real neighbor's dispute. This is all symptomatic of the emotive edge found around decisions about what is inside and outside the boundaries of our territory.

What I want to stress is the unity of a mandala as a whole. The unity of the center, periphery, and their exchange of life-energy is greater than the sum of its parts. The physical world, this spinning ball of earth, constitutes such a mandala. The human body is a mandala, as is every individual cell from which it is made. Mandala principle is a central teaching in the Buddhist tantras, but it has a universal application, and is important at every level of Dharma practice.

8. *Mandala Principle and the Second Truth*

THE BUDDHA'S second truth is concerned with the origin of duhkha—how suffering arises. But where does suffering come from? We find ourselves oppressed by the ego, which narrows our world and creates a closed and sometimes crushing mandala. We can see that suffering comes from continually projecting expectations onto our experience. How and why do we continue putting ourselves into this mess? To answer this question we need to look at the relationship between concepts and emotions.

In the West, we tend to think of emotions and conceptual thought as separate. It might seem worthwhile to investigate the workings of our emotional lives to reduce stress, while any attempt to understand the great issues of life and death sounds like an empty philosophical exercise. Rather than the "love of wisdom," philosophy has come to mean just the use of concepts to understand reality. And there has been a reaction against this toward a more intuitive approach, which has at least this much truth in it: we will never see the real nature of things through concepts alone.

In fact there is a constant play between conceptual structures and emotions. The connection between concepts and the way our emotions work takes the form of a mandala structure. The continuous energy exchange within these structures can be distorted and vampire-like or good and healthy. But in every case, some kind of mandala structure is always in operation.

Part of Buddhist training is to notice the mandala structures operating within and around us all the time. It's easy to assume emotions happen by themselves, in an unstructured fashion, with no thoughts or concepts directing them. But emotions always arise within a mandala structure, whether conceptual or not, and we need to recognize the conceptual connections involved.

Some people claim to work more with emotions than concepts. This is often said to be more true of women than men, but that is just gender propaganda really. Someone may well say, "I work solely on my emotions and feelings!" But when we look more closely and see how angry he or she gets about conceptual things, this is obviously not true.

As a human being you will find yourself using logic regardless of how you feel about it. There is a strong connection between concepts and emotions, and it is the same for both men and women. We use logic all the time, even when we talk about being illogical. We are conceptually driven people, whether we like it or not.

A Weakness for Certain Emotions

We can't avoid using certain basic concepts about the world; this is the way the world presents itself to us. Meanwhile our emotions hover about, waiting for an opportunity to flow down one of the connections created by concepts.

Why do emotions flow more easily in one direction than another? We could fall back on the Buddhist idea of karma and say that past actions create that tendency. We can see this tendency in people's lives, and from a Buddhist point of view this is far more pervasive than we might imagine. If we don't want to go into karma, we could say that some people just have a weakness for certain emotions, and this is what draws them toward certain social mandalas and ways of thinking.

In a very profound sense, all the conceptual frameworks—for hating, desiring, pride, for insensitivity or sensitivity, for loving or not loving—

are excuses for not experiencing emotions directly. Mostly we focus on the effects of our emotions. It's as if we want to view things through the emotion rather than look at the emotion itself. That makes sense, because the basis of any emotion is a way of seeing, even at an enlightened level. But because we aren't awakened, what we see is distorted and probably not worth looking at. Our emotions grab and push us along in an unthinking way, railroading us in certain directions. It would be better to turn around and look at what is propelling us. Otherwise, we are like a dog: the emotion throws a stick and we run after it. Why not turn and face the one who throws the stick instead?

Double Negativity

Generally, we blame the suffering and narrowness of our world on negative emotions like hatred, greed, desire, and insensitivity toward others and ourselves. While that is true, the fault doesn't lie entirely with the emotions.

Trungpa Rinpoche once said that the negativity of the emotions wasn't really a problem. We might find that difficult to believe, but emotions just arise and pass away; they aren't particularly sticky. They are outbursts of energy that first turn one way, then another, on a kind of switchback, but they don't inevitably lead to action. Hatred doesn't necessarily make us kill someone. Likewise desire and the other emotions don't necessarily push us into some negative action. Emotions arise in our bodies, but they don't have to be expressed in external activity.

According to Trungpa Rinpoche, the problem lies in the "negativity of the negativity." This "double negativity" refers to the ideas we have about our emotions, the reasons we give to justify their presence and continuance. Our negative emotions are always associated with some kind of conceptual mandala structure, patterns of thought that can be quite subtle and difficult to recognize. These patterns provide both the trigger and the justification for the emotion, and they are always ego-centered.

We think we hate people because of their particular political persuasion, race, or religion. But actually we just feel hatred and need to indulge it somehow. All our good reasons for hating—and hatred seems to need a good reason—are simply ego's justifications. These fundamentally flawed notions are what Trungpa Rinpoche called "double negativity."

Other Possibilities

There is a strong conceptual link between the arising of an emotion and the physical response. It's worth stressing this because we tend to think mostly in terms of the emotion itself. But the emotion is given a direction by an idea; it wouldn't necessarily give rise to anything by itself. We use concepts to narrow our vision and drive our hatred and desire toward some ego-centered goal.

This narrowing becomes automatic so that, for example, merely to see someone makes us snap at them. At first we may have a reason for our dislike. Maybe we object to their behavior and this drives our hostility, but at some point it all becomes habitual. Whenever we see them we feel hatred and react in an angry way.

In Buddhism a distinction is made between automatic responses and spontaneity, and it is easy to confuse the two. Automatic action is this kind of response. We move from hatred to an angry action with an intermediate concept that flashes by so fast we hardly notice it. The term *spontaneous* describes the way emotions arise and turn toward action when the awakened heart and mind is fully developed. Again, there may not be much apparent thought involved, but the response would be more compassionate and open. The response could appear rather angry but still be compassionate. It could be an energetic way of expressing something that needed to happen. "To nurture what needs to be nurtured, to destroy what needs to be destroyed," as Trungpa Rinpoche used to say.

Hatred is always destructive, but there isn't necessarily anything wrong with that. In the awakened context it has to do with the action of "destroying what needs to be destroyed" in a good and spontaneous way. I must stress that it is very dangerous to think you have reached the stage where you know what needs to be nurtured and what needs to be destroyed. I am simply talking about what is possible. However, it is worth mentioning occasionally because we don't normally look beyond the ordinary way our hatred is expressed or realize there are other possibilities. We look further at the wisdom aspect of hatred in part 3.

Fresh and New

Why does our world feel so closed? It's really a matter of self-preservation. It's difficult to preserve ego, or self, in a truly open environment, where everything is experienced as fresh and new. Buddhist practitioners aspire to experience things in this open way, and the self is gradually eroded by doing that. But what about those who aren't following this path of training?

Every one of us has a certain openness, clarity, and sensitivity. We can't avoid this, but we can certainly limit it. And ego wants to limit it tremendously, to avoid being placed in the position where its boundaries are destroyed. Our ego mandala seems to have a hard boundary, but actually it fluctuates continuously. This notion of a solid boundary is superficially held together by certain ideas we have about ourselves, the world, and the relationship between the two. We identify with our worldview, and we need to address this first.

Hidden Depths

There are several levels of desire, or lust, that drive us. The most superficial—but still powerful—level is the lust for notions and ideas. Human beings passionately espouse and identify with ideas. We think of ourselves as scientists, artists, politicians, good people, bad people, male and female. From these choices we build the mandala of our personal identity. Whenever that identity is threatened, we put up a tremendous fuss.

To know what people identify with, just pick up a newspaper or switch on the television or radio to see what the issues are. Underlying any issue is a passion to identify with something: our family, bloodline, race, political party, or other such things. Then we have the passion for the necessities of life: the need to eat, drink, and have shelter. These are very important, but there are further layers beneath. As we go deeper the issues may sound increasingly theoretical, but they are also profoundly emotional. This is because they connect more directly to what we truly are.

The Fundamental Thirst

The next level is the desire for sensory experience: the thirst to see, feel, smell, taste, and touch. Thirst is a good word to use in this context. We have an overwhelming thirst for air that we never notice unless we have a breathing problem. Our need to breathe is literally a matter of life and death, but our thirst for the world of the senses in general is so tremendously strong that we are overwhelmingly affected by any loss of connection to it. This level of thirst underlies the passion for ideas and notions.

Beneath the desire for sensory experience lies the lust for existence itself. Ordinarily, the most threatening thing we can imagine is serious injury or death. The possibility of ego dissolving away sounds almost an abstraction. But the attachment to existence itself is actually deeper than any attachment to the body.

Finally there is the most fundamental thirst. It lies so deep we are unlikely to recognize it, even when it is talked about. This is the thirst for nonawakening. "I don't want to know things as they truly are!" This is fundamental. We tend to think it is superficial, higher up the chain, but it is way down; it lies beyond even the desire for existence. And it is tremendously emotional, so strongly emotional that it seems more like a constant in our existence. We hold the passion for existence and nonawakening from moment to moment, which is why we can't discern it.

To Be or Not to Be

The second of the Buddha's noble truths addresses the question, where does our duhkha and suffering come from? Duhkha arises from the different levels of thirst and passion. The thirst is caused by an enchantment, an overlay of confusion that goes very deep and covers almost everything that makes up our world. But however deep this overlay may go, it is never complete. It is a mask on reality, and the power of that mask is parasitic. It is a distortion of reality, and when the enchantment disappears, things don't pop into nothingness, like a bubble vanishing. At that point the universe is exposed nakedly and seen as it truly is. In a sense there is no difference between your experience and the universe itself.

Why do we solidify our world and grasp at things with such thirst and passion? Why are our mandalas so closed and narrow instead of open and vast? The basic issue is one of existence versus nonexistence—to be or not to be—and we want to exist! Nonexistence seems almost—but not completely—unthinkable, which is why it is so troubling, and why we flee from it with such emotional intensity. From a Buddhist viewpoint this apparent dilemma is an illusion. We aren't really faced with it, but it's enough that we think we are.

To truly understand this, we need to see how there isn't just one layer of this kind of emotion, with enlightenment immediately beneath it. There is a progression of depths, going right down to the deepest level of confusion—which is associated with tremendous emotionality—until ultimately we pass beyond confusion.

As confusion arises, it comes with its own power, momentum, and mandala structure. The power of that mandala is the basic thirst for existence. This connects to the Buddhist idea of *avidya,* a Sanskrit word which is—somewhat feebly—translated as "ignorance." *Avidya* is not some vagueness that descends upon us. It is actually a volition that precedes any structured sense of self. With ignorance comes a sense of form. Form provides us with something to latch onto, something we can use to pull us up and away from the sense of nonexistence. And from this arises the desire for experience: the desire to work in the world; to smell, taste, touch, move, and breathe; and the sense of an "I" that does all this.

Out of that basis come all our other emotional involvements: the mandalas of my religion, my politics, my race, my parents, my social group; all the things I want to be part of and get so passionate about.

A Question of Classification

The emotions find expression through our passionate involvement in these mandalas. They create channels for our emotions to flow down, and these emotions can be quite complicated. We can see this in ordinary human social structures. Some religions, for example, are structured to channel a kind of charismatic emotion. Some sort of structure is essential—whether it makes sense or not—for the emotion to flow. The devotees of such religions might argue that the form is unimportant, but if the structure isn't right, the emotion won't arise.

These mandala structures can encompass whole groups of people without the need to know anything about particular individuals. Take hatred as an example. Obviously, we try not to hate people on the individual level. But if that were the only reason for hating, 90 percent of the world's hatred would probably disappear. Of course we might occasionally hate a particular individual, but more often it's because they epitomize some notion we have about a specific group or class. Our notions about what these people are like and how they behave is a kind of structure, and we use it to place them inside a mandala.

In the mandala of hatred, the contents become the objects of hatred. What places someone within that mandala? It may be as simple as the belief—conscious or unconscious—that only our group is comprised of truly human beings. Before we can destroy other people we first need to place them outside the mandala of humanness. Once they are shown to be less than fully human, we can harm them as much as we like.

Looking back to the great witch hunts of previous centuries, we see how the victims were first classified as being outside the human mandala. It was the same for heretics, and there are many modern parallels. They were no longer seen as women, men, or children worthy of mercy and compassion. Instead, they became classified as enemies of the human race who could be treated in the most appalling ways. It is just a question of classification. That may sound like a rather cynical remark, but it contains a deep truth.

We need to have the mandala structure in place before we can get the automatic relationship between the beginning and end, between the notions and the emotion. The emotion won't move unless that passage has been created. But once it is accomplished the process can be very quick; it doesn't have to be complicated.

A Club for Hating Foreigners

Our difficulties arise from the passionate longing to identify with ideas and notions about the world. Belonging and excluding go together, so as we enter into a mandala, we exclude whatever doesn't belong within it. This is well illustrated by the English writer who once defined a nation as a "club for hating foreigners."

The commonest reason to develop hatred is the perceived difference between ourselves and others. We may feel so strongly about our notions of religion, race, class, language, or culture that we band together for the sole purpose of rejecting another group and its inimical differences. And we justify this by saying, "They're an assault on our institutions!" or "They don't behave as we do!"

Hatred and paranoia don't exist in themselves. They must have a reason—even if that reason makes no sense—to create the ground for them to run and intensify. We can see people trying to make this happen, supporting each other and telling stories. These could be stories about religion—about Dharma, and gurus, and teachers. There is nothing wrong with any of this, as such; it is quite natural to create such mandalas of connections. But because ignorance is present, it very easily runs into areas where negative emotions build up.

We can espouse and identify with the Buddha's teaching in just as narrow-minded a fashion—even though it runs contrary to the whole thrust of Dharma practice—as we do with anything else. Maybe we find ourselves thinking that other Buddhists aren't really proper practitioners because they don't follow this or that wonderful method. This is bound to happen, simply because we are human, so we need to watch out for it within ourselves as we travel the path.

In Buddhism, no view we take of the universe is true for all time or set in stone. We practice to transcend the view we take of the universe at any given time. As another view becomes appropriate, we train in that view, until we have to abandon that as well.

Finally, we reach the point where we are no longer projecting with a view. We gain some genuine insight that goes beyond reliance on any view as such. Until then, however, we need to see how our views about other people and the world provide the link between our emotions and actions.

The Relationship Mandala

The mandala principle is at work in all relationships between individuals or among members of a group. The mandala of a romantic relationship, for example, would include your beloved and the way you work together in various external situations. The emotional, or internal, aspect of the mandala is the constant energy exchange between you both. Mixed emotions are likely involved, including attachment as well as love. When the external and internal elements are in harmony, the beloved is well within the center of the mandala. However, when the other person—never oneself, of course—acts in a way to make one unhappy, the energy exchange is no longer positive.

It's as though the beloved is approaching some kind of edge. They haven't stepped over it yet, but our antennae tells us they are behaving unexpectedly. We get very emotional about this, which creates the sense of an edge. We become paranoid, fearing that this may become a habit. We worry that our beloved may go on to do things that "go beyond the pale."

Beyond the Pale

It is interesting that the ordinary words we use to describe this are mandala terms. The pale is the boundary, so it is going beyond the edge of the mandala. Strong emotions arise near to this edge, because if it goes too far we could feel both rejected and rejecting. Our feelings could easily change from love to rejection, dislike—even hatred if it went far enough.

So we have a mandala structure associated with desire, a sense of para-noia and emotional transformation as we approach the boundary, and hatred if it passes over the edge. I am dramatizing this, obviously, and relationships can fail without the two parties hating one another. But whatever the outcome, emotionality is central to what happens. A rela-tionship can start as something satisfying and life-enhancing but become something altogether different when the boundary is crossed.

The structure of a relationship mandala is associated with our behav-ior, the things we say and do. These are not especially emotional in them-selves, they are just words, actions, and the expression of concepts. However, they trigger emotions because of the links between thoughts, words, actions, and our expectations.

Our egocentricity always expresses itself in two ways: the mandala structures and the emotions connected with them. Nearly everything con-nected with ego comes from the dynamic play between these two.

The main task in the Buddha's second truth is to see how these nega-tive mandala structures operate, and how they push us into actions of body, speech, and mind. We need to look at the conceptual bridges between our emotions and the way we give vent to them.

9. The Mandala of Openness

THE GENERAL PRINCIPLE in mindfulness practice is to be as open and as aware as possible. It is the basis of all the various methods for breaking down conceptual structures, which is why it is pushed so hard at the beginning. Trungpa Rinpoche always stressed the attitude of being completely open to every situation that arises, whatever it is, without judging it. He introduced various special techniques at different times, but the basic practice was always this training in openness.

The Mandala of Meditation

In the mandala of formless meditation, you are the center of your world. This is a very spacious feeling, if you relax into it properly. As you sit with eyes partly open, in a relaxed and stable posture, any feeling of clutter around you disappears. You may even become slightly apprehensive as this sense of spaciousness becomes stronger. Mostly we are not used to being in the center of our worlds in such a spacious way. But just relax into the space. You don't need eyes in the back of your head; the universe isn't going to stab you in the back. Just rest confidently in openness and awareness.

The Breath-Body

You are in the center of a mandala of space that is potentially boundless. This could be a wonderful feeling. Theoretically, we know that space goes on forever, but we tend to think of it stopping at the four walls around us. Even while sitting outside under a tree, we have the notion of a great blue dome that is vast but still limited. Once we notice the sense of limitation we can give it up. After all, it is just another notion. The only reason we don't let go is a fear of space itself.

As we saw in chapter 3, the basic reference point in this meditation is the out-breath. When we breathe out, we let go into the space around us. But we aren't pushing back a boundary. It is more a case of letting go of any notion of boundaries altogether. The in-breath has a natural quality of relaxation that helps with this. The mandala we are working with here is the mandala of our personal space, which is associated with the physical body.

The inside of this mandala is the "breath-body" and outside that mandala is the spacious world around you. The boundary is the gap between the in- and out-breath. Trungpa Rinpoche talked about the emotionality underlying this boundary. Breathing in requires some effort, so as we breathe out there is always the concern: "Will I be able to breath in again?" This is a very emotional issue, but at such a subtle level that we rarely notice it because we are so used to the experience. In meditation, we defuse any possible sense of problem by relaxing on the in-breath.

The mandala of meditation is a dynamic process in which the out-breath flows from the inside of the mandala to the endless spaciousness outside. And we are being quite courageous when we breathe in. I wouldn't want to make anyone paranoid, but who knows what's out there! Of course, this is another non-issue from the ordinary point of view. Nevertheless, there is something strangely warrior-like involved in breathing in and out. This may sound silly. We've been breathing all our lives, so how could there be anything significant in that? But there is, we just never notice or recognize it.

One Seamless Web

It would be wonderful if we could simply meditate on the breath. Why would you need to bother about the mind? Well, it may come as a surprise, but the mind doesn't do what it's told. You decide to meditate on the breath, and it's as if your mind says, "A likely story!" Working with the breath is easy enough at the beginning because it has the great virtue of novelty. But, as we noted above, it soon becomes boring, and all kinds of thoughts start popping up.

When this happens we could try to thrust all thoughts out of our mind, but this doesn't work and is not recommended. Nor is there any point in following the trains of thought that arise, which is what we ordinarily do.

The best approach to follow is the one Trungpa Rinpoche described, where you treat the thoughts, feelings, and emotions that arise as guests arriving at a party. You are a good host who greets all the guests with equal attentiveness. By "greeting" he meant allowing yourself to feel and experience them as clearly as possible, with a minimum of judgmental thoughts; then let them go and return to the breath. You never need think of them as interruptions. They are all part of the meditation practice, part of the dance of your mind.

In time, you can develop some real skill in attending to the breath, dealing with whatever comes into your mind, and switching back to the breath. It may be rather jerky at first, but eventually you learn how to move quickly and smoothly from one to the other. There can be a sense of speed and accuracy, without letting anything slip, while feeling totally relaxed at the same time.

Relating to thoughts and feelings in this way is another kind of mandala. Take the attitude that it's all one seamless web. Any interrupting thoughts and feelings are part of the meditation. As they come into our minds, they enter the mandala of our meditation practice.

Nothing is excluded from the mandala of meditative practice, which is greater than the mandala of ordinary experience. In ordinary experience, certain things are permitted but others are thrust outside. If they try to force their way in, we push them away. We can become so expert at this that we don't even notice them knocking at the door. In the mandala of meditation, we train to be open to everything that arises, through the process of awareness and openness.

The emotional aspect arises on the boundary where we greet our guests. Until we are adept at this process, we easily fall into ordinary emotional habit patterns, reacting for-or-against. When this happens, don't think, "That was a bad move!" Just notice the reaction of accepting or rejecting and consider it as part of the meditation. Once you get a feel for this, nothing will get past you.

It's interesting how we adopt these judgmental feelings as "me" rather than seeing them as just another object of mind. They seem so very special that we can't treat them as just another thought. But in fact that's exactly what they are. Recognizing this is a necessary first step toward removing their power of ego-centered specialness. Obviously, there are many subtleties to this, but learning how it all works is part of the meditative process. And that process starts when we stop treating them as special.

Anxiety and Confidence

A sense of anxiety arises as we practice because the apparent solidity of our selves and our world has begun to unravel. It's like trying to cross a river on stepping stones: we fear to move from one stone because we're not sure we can reach the next. This is where confidence, or certainty, comes in.

Confidence is strangely "beyond hope and fear," as Trungpa Rinpoche once said. Interestingly, it is not about relying on oneself, which is just as well given how feeble one is much of the time. It's about relying on the intrinsic quality of openness and clarity that is our real being, beyond self. Sometimes we need to be put into situations where there is no other choice, where openness is the only way to go simply because every other possibility is closed off. That's why the path of openness can be a bit scary at times.

A Better Kind of Stability

As we relate to the sense of space all around and beneath us, it's possible to feel like we're flying, and however much we try to find a stable position on the meditation cushion, we still feel odd. However, there is more than one kind of stability.

Some people have a stolid kind of stability. This has nothing to do with Dharma; they are just naturally "pudding-like." They aren't stupid particularly, but they sit in a heavy kind of way and aren't much affected by their emotions. We might call this a poor man's version of stability.

On the path of Buddhadharma, we are trying to reach a better kind of stability, one that's associated with the mind being awake. In the initial stages of awakening we realize the world is considerably more shaky, impermanent, and less graspable than it seemed. Things seem to be dissolving all around us, and consequently we don't feel especially stable. The beginning stages of Buddhist practice don't seem to make for a more stable mind, but strangely enough, our practice is moving in that direction.

It's like we've been floating around on a raft in a lake, with the shore a long way off. This raft could become wrecked or waterlogged and drop out from under us at any time. As long as we don't think about it, it seems quite stable, and we feel happy where we are; we don't even realize there is a solid shore to reach. But once the blinkers are off we feel an urgent need to find a way of getting to shore.

The problem is that we have realized the instability of our world and glimpsed a reality that is genuinely stable, but we still have to make the transition from one to the other. It is quite possible that we will feel even less stable while we make that transition. Traveling from where we are now to what is real is never going to be "roses, roses all the way"; the Buddha himself said there would be problems and difficulties. We are living in what Buddhists call *samsara*, or conditioned existence, which is an ocean of suffering. Things might not seem too bad in our personal bit of samsara just at the moment, but that won't last forever, and who knows what might happen next.

The Buddha's message points to the instability of it all, and in that sense it is destabilizing. Suddenly we no longer feel quite so safe. But the genuine stability we seek is not so easy to come by. It involves working sensibly with this natural instability of things.

A Natural Allegiance

As Dharma practitioners, we often have to bring together seemingly paradoxical things. Sometimes we work with the sense of boundless space around us. At other times, we work to feel the stability of the earth beneath us. This isn't earth as such, but a symbol for the quality that supports and sustains, which is also a quality of space. And we have to work with both. We need the stable confidence that we are in the center of our world, even though we are surrounded by boundless space in all directions.

When we experience the ground as space-like, it may very well feel like we are floating. This is just one of the many meditative experiences—*nyams* in Tibetan—that may arise as we practice. This particular nyam of space, or emptiness, is not a proper experience of emptiness itself; it is a spin-off effect that comes from moving in that direction.

Another kind of nyam may occur when we realize we don't make volitions happen; they arise of themselves. This nyam can make us feel suddenly powerless and lead to a kind of paranoia. We feel that we ought to be the one who makes things happen. Eventually we realize that it was never like that. All our actions are spontaneous, if we could but see it.

This is all very unsettling, but Buddhist practice offers no insurance against feeling strange. It would be very surprising if you didn't feel strange, in one way or another, because anything unsettling to ego feels strange. But as we practice, we are moving toward a greater stability, which rests on awareness and confidence in space itself.

That final stability might be some way off. But you could have a flash experience at any time: as an inspiration, an intuition, or a sudden revelation about the remarkable nature of the space around you—the amazing fact that space is connected with the truth itself. Buddhist practitioners have practiced like this for 2,500 years and more, and a great many people from very different cultures have experienced the same unsettling things.

If it is all so disturbing and unsettling, why do people follow this path? The answer is that these meditative experiences may not be the ultimate truth, but they do lead in a direction that has more truth to it than where we normally stand. When we ask ourselves those fundamental questions about the nature of existence, we really want to know the truth. Human beings seem to have a natural allegiance to truth, and that's why we continue to practice, however unsettling it may be.

Self-Secret

The practice of openness is simple enough to explain and, in principle, not that difficult to apply. As we go on we will find subtleties, depths, and vastness in the practice of openness that we never imagined were possible. But it is simple, even at the highest level it is simple. It's we who are complicated.

It would be a bit unkind to say "Be open," without giving something more. But it's amazing how far we can go with just the simple phrase "be open." But why is this? We are so accustomed to words working in this way that we never question it. The door in front of me is open, space is open, but why can we use words figuratively? Words have a power in them that we might never suspect. They connect our minds and emotions with the world.

Trungpa Rinpoche taught us to rely on the quality of openness. This is a method that belongs to the highest level of the tantras and goes beyond the usual tantric techniques. It is a tremendously helpful practice and way of relating to life, which will stay with you throughout your Buddhist career—even haunt you—right up until enlightenment. And it can be taught openly, right from the beginning, because it is "self-secret."

Many of the powerful tantric techniques aren't taught until later on, or are couched in mysterious ways, because they can create considerable power, and there is always the danger this could be misused in some way. That is why there is a tremendous emphasis on developing awareness and compassion; to be "kind to yourself and merciful toward others." We have to learn compassion in both directions, toward both ourselves and others, before being introduced to these powerful methods.

The practice of openness is self-secret because we simply can't understand its real meaning until much later. Nonetheless, it is always helpful, at whatever level we do understand it.

The Maṇḍala of Everyday Life

We are always the center of the mandala of our world, the mandala of "me and mine." This mandala includes all the things we can control or manipulate and consider to be ours. The boundary consists of those areas of uncertainty, where our control is not certain.

Central to this mandala are the emotions of grasping and rejecting. Looking around us, we find certain things we want to attract or seduce into our world and other things we want to reject. Looking at ourselves, there are certain qualities we want to exclude or remove, and others we'd like to acquire and incorporate. It is always a big emotional issue when things are crossing the boundary of our mandala, in either direction. This is the mandala of our ordinary life, which has egocentricity as its central principle. How does this compare to the mandala of openness?

In the mandala of openness, we make awareness the central principle, with the quality of openness suffusing the mandala as a whole. This is the basic teaching of the Buddha: to be open to every situation that arises. However, this doesn't mean we should open ourselves to anything and everything, in a haphazard fashion. Openness is always mediated through genuine awareness and sensitivity. We allow whatever situations arise, pleasant or unpleasant, to come toward us. We feel the situation without shrinking away or making judgments about whether it's good or bad.

In the mandala of openness we turn toward situations, experience them clearly, and let them go. Their emotional force is quite different when we do this. They don't obsess us in the way negative experiences often do. When we dread a certain event, for example, we probably think and worry

about it a lot. We play around with different scenarios, imagining ourselves making our usual responses, desperately trying to find something
that works. Unfortunately, all we have to fall back on are our old patterns, and we can find ourselves replaying the same unpleasant scenario
over and over again. We never experience anything fresh.

The quality of openness introduces something new to the situation—
both in formal meditation sessions and everyday life—and brings another
dimension to our experience.

The Dangers of Openness

The practice of openness might bring with it the danger of some emotional disturbance. But this has never been considered a good reason for
not meditating or opening yourself out. If anything, it is a reason for developing more openness and awareness.

People can fall into one of two extremes. There are those who push
things away and never allow anything new into their lives; and those who
allow almost anything, even the most abusive or crazy things, into their
world. This kind of unrestricted openness is crude and chaotic. It is not
real openness and has nothing to do with meditation.

In genuine meditation, awareness is at the center of our mandala, and
we bring awareness to whatever comes into our minds. So long as we
relate to whatever arises through awareness, nothing that expresses itself
is ever a problem. The things we allow in won't turn round and put the
knife into us, as they might if we were chaotically open.

Disturbing Realizations

A great teacher was once teaching a meditation on emptiness, which
lessens the habit of grasping at things as real. During this teaching, a student grabbed hold of his clothes with both hands. After the talk he said
to the teacher, "I felt as if I'd disappeared. I grabbed at myself, but there
was nothing to hold on to but external things, like my clothes." He was

terrified by this experience of emptiness. It is a natural defensive reaction to cling onto something. And because there is no concrete self to hold on to, we grasp at whatever comes to hand, in an effort to "pull ourselves together!"

The teacher explained to the student that the reason his experience was frightening was because it was only a partial realization of emptiness. Had it been complete, he wouldn't have felt afraid. Nevertheless, it was a good experience, because the student had at least some partial realization of the truth.

It is important to have an experienced teacher and a community of practitioners around us when this starts to happen. However unsettling such a partial realization may be, we may also find that meditation allows us to relate to all those difficult—but ordinary—life experiences that we can't cope with now.

Ultimately, the reason we continue to meditate through painful or frightening experiences is because we realize it's about truth. This is not truth in a conceptual sense. The truth is attractive and seductive, and although it can be scary, it pulls us along. How far does the realization of emptiness go? How far does the scariness extend? Are there any limits? Tradition says it can go quite a long way. So should we be worried about having unpleasant experiences? I don't think we should.

Meditating doesn't insure us against unpleasantness, any more than not meditating does. We are all going to die at some point, and that is unlikely to be pleasant. It might be comforting to think we will only experience the scary aspects of openness when we're ready for them. However, it doesn't seem to work like that. We can experience something long before we become stable in it. This may be disturbing, but it's a dangerous old world, whether we meditate or not, isn't it?

Stepping Outside

Mahayana Buddhism has many techniques for dissolving egocentric mandala structures. We can use analysis to convince us of the emptiness of the concepts that hold them together. Alternatively, we can work to dissolve them by training in openness. We can train to notice when an emotion is pushing or propelling us from behind, and to recognize that it's just another feeling. We then see how problems arise whenever we identify with some thought or feeling and adopt it as special.

If we investigate, for example, our reasons for disliking a certain group or community, we find that the underlying conceptual structures can be eroded away quite easily. So why are they so powerful? It's because at some point we have strongly identified with a particular social mandala and way of thinking. There is a constant energy exchange between you and the other members of the mandala that reinforces these ideas and allows them to continue.

How can we step outside such a mandala? These people are probably our friends. We identify with the group and it gives us a sense of support. We say things like, "My people are behind me!" But what we really mean is they propel us from behind. We don't have to think for ourselves because we are part of the group.

We have a lot to give up should we leave that group: friendship, companionship, and the many kinds of energy exchange and feedback that goes along with it. These are the things that hold us in place. It's like we are plumbed into the mandala. We find ourselves completely immersed in the situation, and this is why the second truth is such a difficult area to work with.

You can experiment with this, just to get the feeling of being outside a mandala that you really identify with. There wouldn't be much point in a Christian trying to imagine what it is like to no longer be a Buddhist. But a Christian could imagine being thrown out of the Christian mandala and how that would feel.

Take another example. Let's say you have a very loving family. Then one day you go home and find your house has disappeared, your family is gone, and no one has ever heard of you. You might say, "That could never happen!" Well it could happen, if only in your imagination. Are you afraid to imagine such a thing? Would it be tempting fate? Thinking like this makes us restive because it feels almost too uncomfortable to contemplate.

Imagining something like this can be helpful, because while there is genuine love and real connection involved, there is also a lot of attachment. It is good to get the feel of being in such a different world. If our imagination is vivid enough, we can get some sense of the power these mandalas have over us. They don't have quite the power of the constant lust for existence, but it's because we are so immersed in them that we find it so difficult to distinguish attachment, mere connection, and genuine love.

Assuming you are very close to your parents, imagine how it would feel to lose them. Without destroying your good feelings for them, just explore what it would be like to lose your parents. If you feel it's a real problem even to play with this possibility, it might good to investigate why that is. I remember, when I was young, traveling home on the bus from school and wondering, "What if I get home and find there's no house there?"

The point here is to get a sense of the power these mandalas have over us by playing with how it would feel to be outside one of these fundamental mandalas. It can open up a new dimension in our experience.

Enlightenment and the Great Cosmic Soup

Of course, we won't solve everything by removing ourselves from these mandalas. If we move out of one mandala we simply find ourselves in another. The whole world is made up of interlocking mandalas; they are found everywhere. There is no point in trying to get rid of mandalas. What we need is to learn how to discriminate between negative and positive mandalas and understand how they work.

What's more, mandalas don't vanish at enlightenment. Instead, they operate spontaneously, rather than in the solid way they appear to us now. Enlightenment doesn't mean everything dissolves away into some great cosmic soup, or featureless vastness. It may be vast beyond thought, awe-inspiring, and astonishing, but it still has some kind of structure. Enlightenment isn't bounded by concepts and can't be definitively described in words, but insofar as anything can be said at all, the mandala principle probably offers the best description.

PART 3. THE COLLAPSE OF CONFUSION

& The Cessation of Suffering

"These our actors,
As I foretold you, were all spirits, and
Are melted into air, into thin air;
And, like the baseless fabric of this vision,
The cloud-capp'd towers, the gorgeous palaces,
The solemn temples, the great globe itself,
Yea, all which it inherit, shall dissolve,
And, like this insubstantial pageant faded,
Leave not a rack behind."
—William Shakespeare, *The Tempest*

There are ways of meditating that reveal the falsity of our ordinary views of past, present, and future, of the nature of place, and even of the existence of objects in the world. We could live out our whole lives and never question these fundamental concepts, and most people do just that.

10. On Time

AT THE LEVEL of the Buddha's third truth, the key word is *cessation*: the cessation of our clinging to conceptual structures and the emotions that run through them. We need to work with each of these—the concepts and the emotions—separately, in a kind of two-pronged attack.

In the second truth we looked at the conceptual structures that form a channel for our desire, hatred, and paranoia. In these next two chapters we will look at concepts that seem so fundamental that they are never questioned. There are ways of meditating that reveal the falsity of our ordinary views of past, present, and future, of the nature of place, and even of the existence of objects in the world. We could live out our whole lives and never question these fundamental concepts, and most people do just that. The Buddhist challenge is to look directly at these things that are so basic we never question them. We then get to see just how shaky they are.

In the second prong of the attack, we look at the nature of emotions— what they are in themselves—rather than taking them for granted. What is an emotion? It is possible to find the answer as a direct personal experience. If you can't, then nobody else can do it for you. Ultimately, you can't rely on what it says in this or that book. The best a teacher can do is to give a new and unexpected way of looking at things: in this case a tool for looking directly at the nature of your emotions. We investigate the emotions in chapters 12 and 13.

The Ground We Stand Upon

Up until now we have been able to categorize our lives in terms of the three times—past, present, and future. This holds up well enough until we look at it more closely. The Buddhist way of looking at phenomena says that the experience of past, present, and future is like *maya,* a magical illusion. It's as though the trick of the three times has been played on us all. It turns out that the world is an extremely dynamic place, and our experience is not as fixed or given as we think.

It's important to stress just how emotionally shocking it is to see the falseness of our old vision of the world; to recognize, for example, that we hold on to the notion of past, present, and future literally like "grim death." Whenever we puncture any one of these very basic notions, we find ourselves faced with a life-and-death situation. They are like the ground we stand upon, and it's as if we are projected into space as the earth beneath us collapses.

Our whole lives are built on such notions as past, present, and future. And when we discover they are merely a conceptual construction, it's as though our very lives are threatened. It is good to be brought up short, to realize that we've had these wrong ways of thinking for so long. But once this revelation hits home, the question arises, "When did it ever begin?" It's like we have been making these strange projections onto the world forever, and now, suddenly, everything is different.

We may have started on the path by wondering about the meaning of existence, questioning whether life has any point, or why anything exists at all. Now we realize that there may even be something false in the way we pose these fundamental questions. Merely to see this is a kind of revelation, and it links to our natural sense of truth.

The meditations I am now going to describe are powerful means for collapsing the false projections we make on our experience. To be of any real value they require further personal instruction and the support of a suitably experienced teacher. If you don't have such support, it is best to consider this as a connection that will allow you to begin practicing these meditations when the circumstances are right.

Collapsing the Three Times

Time is probably the easiest fundamental structure to begin with. The meditation is very simple and is based on the formless meditation practice outlined earlier. Here, however, it isn't necessary to meditate on the breath. You can just relax and let your mind wander a little.

In next to no time you will be thinking about the past, because that's what we always do. When I say "past" I mean anything you remember, whether it's something from five years ago or something from this morning. Such thoughts continually come into our minds. Alternatively we wonder about tomorrow; we project into the future, and based on our past experiences, imagine how it might be.

As thoughts about the past come into our minds, it's important to realize that we are not literally in the past. Of course, if we were challenged, we would probably say we are remembering something in the present moment. But there is a flavor of what we might call "pastness" to the experience that makes us lose the sense of being in the present. It feels like we are actually conveyed into the past.

In this practice we remain our normal, uncritical selves. We allow ourselves to become completely immersed in any memories that arise. At that point we can then wake ourselves up by realizing that whatever happens is taking place *now* and not in the past; it is a present experience. Any experience of the past happens now. And the same goes for any projected experience of the future.

The Past

When all is said and done, we find ourselves alone with our memories. So how do we know they are real? Normally we feel we're quite good at making such judgments, and we can cross-reference the evidence with others when necessary. Occasionally our memories turn out to be false or imagined, but generally the world and our memories seem to hang together and make some kind of sense.

What makes us confident that a memory is genuine? It's because it possesses a quality or flavor of pastness that convinces us. But when does that conviction happen? It happens in the present. Again, this is unsurprising. Everything we experience has to be experienced now. It makes no sense to say that we experience the past. Whenever we think of the past, it is a direct and present experience.

Things from the past feel lost to us. We relate to them as memories, which, as far as we are concerned, is all they are. The conviction of pastness is the vehicle that carries us back into a memory and makes it seem like we are reliving the past. We can't deny this conviction, but it, too, happens in the present and nowhere else. Any sense of the past and experience of memory always happens now.

Nowness is the essence and criteria of our experience. It's where everything happens and includes all notions about being in a particular time or place. We can't really lose ourselves in the past if we take this view, and it's not difficult to see that this would be equally true of the future.

One interesting spin-off from this experience is that the solidity of the past breaks down. Normally, we think the past is solid and unchangeable, like a mountain. We might look back into the past to see how we got into our present situation. We may think about changing our behavior to create something better for the future. But we never think we can do anything about the past. The past seems monolithic and untouchable. In one sense, the past seems to be alive, because we can seemingly re-live experiences. In another sense, it seems as dead and fixed as a butterfly pinned to a card; something that has only the appearance of life.

So our past is like a collection of beautiful, but dead, butterflies. It might be attractive or repulsive, but there is nothing we can do about it. And there is something sad about this. Certainly as we get older, we may regret things from the past, but we don't feel we can do anything about that. It's just something we are stuck with.

Since this sense of pastness is all in the present, however, we *can* do something with it. I won't go so far as to say we can change the past, but we could certainly transform our attitude toward it. When we see that the past is always contained within the dynamic present, it no longer seems dead and monolithic. The past becomes a living, present experience, rather than the familiar fossilized rock of old.

The Future

When we think about the future, we don't believe we are actually in the future. We think of it as a projection of the future, a projection with a particular flavor. It may or may not ever happen, but any projection of how the future might be always happens in the present and nowhere else.

Whenever we wonder about how things might turn out in the future—with all our hopes, expectations, fears, and associated anxieties—this happens now, and not in some probable, problematic future. The imagined future is something we are creating at this moment; it appears directly before us. Once we see this, we realize—and this is true of nearly all Buddhist teaching—that it is completely obvious. We might wonder why it's necessary to say anything at all. The reason is equally simple: while these things may be obvious, we happily ignore them and act as though they weren't true.

The Power of the Present

Now you might wonder what the word *present* could mean. If we continually point out to ourselves that the past and future happen in the present, where exactly is this present? Our idea of the present is sandwiched between the past and the future, which creates a problem, because the past and the future are always experienced now.

By meditating in this way, the reality of the past disappears into the dynamism of the present moment. The future is absorbed into the present as well. And since the present is only defined in terms of past and future, at that point, the word *present* ceases to have any meaning.

All our sense of power and ability to change—and to affect, to be aware, and so on—is in the present. The past, for instance, is a living, present experience; something we can encounter and almost have a real conversation with, in the sense that something could change from both sides. The past is not stuck and fossilized. Any sense of powerlessness that goes with the past is completely contradicted by the presentness of the experience.

Since we are always in the present, we have more power than we think. But we have forgotten this. How can we wake ourselves out of the sense of being in the past when we are totally immersed in it? Some people can do this spontaneously: they can wake themselves up simply through their commitment to the practice. For others it happens more gradually; and the recognition of having tried and failed reminds them to make a more focused effort in the future. If you have an underlying wish to understand and connect to this, sooner or later you will succeed.

By practicing in this way, the past and future are reduced to the present; and—because we have removed the very things that define it—the present isn't anywhere. So where, in time, are our experiences? Practicing like this doesn't remove the completeness of our experience; it only removes our normal view of the three times: the monolithic past; the thin—but all-important—slice of the present; and our projections and fantasies about the future. Seeing clearly the immediacy of our experience of past, future, and present, if only for a moment, collapses the three times, and they disappear. The new experience that is presented to us can't be categorized in terms of the three times. We could call it immediacy, now-ness, presentness, or some other newly invented jargon, but this just disguises the fact that we don't really know what it is. However we describe the experience, it certainly isn't past, present, or future in the ordinary sense.

Meditation as Medicine

Two problems need to be mentioned regarding this meditation. Some practitioners find it incredibly difficult to relate to the experience of past, present, and future in anything but a theoretical way. This is not what the meditation is about at all. Rather than being a theoretical investigation, this meditation is about experiencing the three times as "now" and undercutting our emotionally held notions about past, present, and future. Some people find this difficult, and their practice always remains at an intellectual level. A few find it easy, while many others grow into it gradually.

The second problem lies in the question: how can we go on living when the past and future are experienced in the present and the present doesn't exist? And do we have to do this practice all the time? The answer is both yes and no. We have to meditate like this in order to experience the collapse of the three times. The truth of this should be obvious, but it isn't, because of the way we cling to notions of past, present, and future. This clinging creates a distortion that makes it difficult to see things clearly.

Generally speaking, Buddhist meditation techniques are medicines that address particular issues, so we don't have to go on doing the same meditation for ever afterward. The meditation we do at twenty may well be different to the one we practice at forty. When the time is right, your teacher will probably tell you to move on to another practice.

The process of uncovering and collapsing the structure of the three times sounds a bit like going back to childhood, to when we first built the grammar of perception. But from a Buddhist point of view there is much more to it than that. We don't come into this world with all the right stuff only to find it all goes wrong as we grow up. We have always been wrong.

The problem is we don't want to give up the past. It contains all our endeavors, ambitions, and wishes for the future. We've done so much, worked so hard, and made so many mistakes, surely there must be something to it? We could awaken right now, at this very moment, and become like a child again, seeing everything as fresh and new, without that almost infinite filtration of past experience. But first we would have to give up all our past.

As we get a glimpse of this possibility, there is a very strong, almost childish, reaction: "I can't give up everything I did in the past! It must be real!" So there is a choice between the childishness that says, "I'm not going to give it up!" and a genuinely childlike response, where we let go of our clinging and see everything clearly and freshly.

Of Children and Animals

In a famous poem, children are described as "trailing clouds of glory" as they emerge from the heaven that they return to when they die. It's the idea that children come into the world completely pristine and unsullied. This is not a Buddhist way of thinking. Children most likely come from a place just like our own. And if they did come from some kind of heaven, there would be nothing special in that. It's just another part of samsara. Children are basically underdeveloped. Their confusion isn't yet fully developed, and it's this quality that makes them appear innocent.

The Buddha said that while children don't possess the fully developed sense of ego that adults have, the potential is there and will develop in the future. Similarly, their perceptual structures are not yet solid. Their sense of subject and object is a bit more fluid. Very small children are uncertain about what is, or isn't, "me." But this isn't particularly wonderful; adults can have the same experience when they're very sick, and it doesn't make them enlightened.

The sharp, spacious quality of mind of the awakened ones is not possessed by children or sick people suffering from confused perceptions. So let's forget about clouds of glory. Children need adults to bring them up. Hopefully the adults do this without imposing too many of their own prejudices on the children. And maybe the adults could use that apparent innocence as a pointer toward something more genuine.

Animals are often seen as innocent and pure in much the same way. They may not have many of our problems, but this is simply because they don't have all of our human capacities. A woman once told me that her highly intelligent cat had special characteristics that made it better than a human being. I begged to differ. Human beings have many more qualities than animals. These qualities may have many defects, but that's only because we aren't sufficiently awakened. So, as Trungpa Rinpoche might have put it: it is my duty to tell you that you are all potential kings and queens of awakening—not babies, and still less cats!

Coming Out the Other Side

At some point in our practice, we get to the point where things collapse. It's only through experiencing the death-like quality of that collapse that we get the real message of "presentness." In the dzogchen teachings of

Buddhism this is sometimes referred to as the *fourth time*. This is just a way of talking about experience after all our clinging to the three times is removed. There are other names for this, but fourth time is nice and neutral. Interestingly, it doesn't tell us anything about time, as such. It is not saying that everything is present, because there is no present. Indeed, they sometimes say there were never even words such as past, present, or future as a way of hammering home the power of this truth.

Even when we've experienced things in terms of the fourth time, it doesn't suddenly become impossible to talk about the past, present, and future. It might well be useful or necessary to do this. However, our attitude to the three times is completely different. Buddhists talk a lot about such things as non-self and collapsing time and place. But the Buddha—who had realized non-self and freedom from the three times—was still happy to refer to himself as "I" and to speak in terms of yesterday, tomorrow, and today.

Through meditation we undermine the clinging that distorts and twists our experience in such a profound way. The collapse of our false notions about the world is both terrifying and undermining, but as we gradually learn to relate to the experience, it changes us, and eventually we come out the other side. The world becomes transformed, not as some kind of theory but as a direct experience. Past, present, and future come to have a totally different value and meaning, and everything is experienced in a brighter, more vivid, and more truthful way.

11. On Place

Having looked at time, we can now investigate the nature of place. One way to do this is to ask direct questions about thoughts: Where do thoughts come from? Where are they when they appear before us? And where do they go when they disappear?

Too Simple and Too Obvious

Many students find this meditation even more difficult than meditating on the three times. When you ask yourself "Where do thoughts come from?" you may instantly reply, "Thoughts come from my mind." This is not helpful, because "my mind" is just words, and we are not looking for words. We are looking for a direct experience. We habitually say that thoughts come from the mind, even though we have no idea what we mean by it. We talk about "my mind" all the time, without having the faintest idea what it is! So it means nothing to say that thoughts are in my mind. And to say, as people often do these days, that thoughts come from the subconscious or unconscious is just as unclear and meaningless. *Mind* is just a word. We need to look for the place where thoughts arise as an actual experience.

The problem is that what we are being asked to do is too simple. One of the main difficulties with Buddhist practice is that it is too simple and too obvious. We human beings are very complicated, and we like theoretical structures. We don't want to look at things in a simple, straightforward way and ask ourselves such direct questions.

If you hold a glass of orange juice in your hand and ask yourself, "Where did this glass come from?" it would make sense to say that it was created by a glassmaker or some kind of machine. You could then consider the elaborate conditions that produced the glass. But it's quite a different matter when you are talking about your own mind.

Where Are We Now?

To answer the question "Where do thoughts come from," we need to look at our own direct experience. For example, let's say that while you are doing this practice, a pop song is running through your mind. To argue that this song arose because you heard it before is like saying the drinking glass comes from the glass maker. In other words, there is an association between the two, but this doesn't answer the question we are asking.

The moment something arises in your mind—be it a pop song, an emotion, a feeling—look directly at this seemingly completely fresh appearance, and without conceptual thought, ask yourself where it comes from. Look directly at the place where it arises. Does it come from anywhere?

I could just stop there and leave it to you, but there is no problem in telling you the answer. Except, in some sense it isn't really an answer, because you still have to see it for yourself. The answer is very simple: thoughts don't come from anywhere. When a thought comes into your mind, it comes from nowhere whatsoever. And when it disappears, it doesn't go anywhere. There is no mental store or elephant's graveyard of thoughts; it just disappears and ceases to exist.

So what does it mean to say that thoughts, feelings, and perceptions appear in front of us? Imagine you and I are sitting in a meeting room in Oxford, having this conversation. Ordinarily we think that all this appearance happens immediately before us. But where is that? Where are all these thoughts, feelings, and perceptions? Your direct experience is not just the things you can see, hear, smell, taste, or touch; there are also your thoughts about Oxford, and the meeting room, and about me sitting there in front of you. All these ideas could also be considered to be appearing before you. But the notion of Oxford, the meeting room, or of any place whatsoever, is simply another experience, or another thought. It can't be the case that they happen in Oxford. There is no "here" apart from a construction I make out of sense perceptions and mind.

So where are all these sense perceptions, feelings, and notions about such things as Oxford and in-front-ness located? The answer—and this is a direct and immediate experience—is they aren't anywhere. Where are we now? We are nowhere.

Powerful Medicine

This is not some strange esoteric meditation; it is simply common sense. Any sense of place—London, New York, Oxford—is built on sense perceptions, concepts, and thoughts, which we experience as a complete package. The notion of place begins to collapse when we realize that this complete package isn't anywhere.

Place is a relative notion. When we investigate the nature of place more deeply, it collapses in the same way that past, present, and future collapse. Everything we saw to be true of past, present, and future—and our difficulties relating to that—can equally be said about place. Many people find this practice difficult, and wonder whether we're simply playing with words. But it isn't a matter of tricky language; you just have to pick your way through it.

Are we saying, then, that there is no such thing as place? Well, in fact, we could go further. We could pursue the notion of objects, and show that from this point of view, there aren't any objects either. Are we saying there really aren't any objects? The answer is: yes! By meditating in this way, you will see there are no objects or places.

It is necessary to do this because of the fundamentally wrongheaded way we relate to experience. We have to unpick the seams of our emotional clinging and the way we identify with things in such an untruthful way. Ultimately we might be able to say more about the true nature of experience, of perceptions, of thoughts, of apparent objects, and so on. At the moment, however, we all suffer from this same mental affliction, so we all need to take the medicine. Once the disease is cured the medicine will no longer be needed. But even though it's just a device, and by no means the last word, this is very powerful medicine indeed.

The Collapse of the World as We Know It

All these meditations lead us to more or less the same place: the collapse of the world as we know it. There are different routes to this, but somewhere along the way, we will get a flash experience of the collapse of the three times, the collapse of place, or the collapse of objects. There are actually many methods we could use. We have focused on space and time because they are so obviously fundamental.

While all these meditations are very unsettling—it can seem like the world is collapsing around our ears—amazingly, we can live through this experience and come out the other side. And when we do, we won't be the same. Something will have changed in us. We will still be able to use words like Oxford, London, or New York and make sense to others, but the words will no longer have the same meaning or emotional value. Our vision and outlook has changed.

Memory and Déjà Vu

In this context, you may wonder about memory and déjà vu. Most of us have had experiences of déjà vu. We might go to a place we haven't visited for a long time and find the same people, doing and saying the same old things, and we have a tremendous sense of déjà vu.

A student once told me about reading a story to her children some forty years after it was read to her. She hadn't thought about this story over the intervening decades and was struck to find it completely familiar. She wondered whether there is some kind of storehouse where all our experiences are stored so that nothing is ever forgotten. Would this account for the claims that at the moment of death we see our lives flashing before our eyes?

The true reality of things is beyond explanation or any kind of conceptual framework. Overlaying that reality is the confused picture of our self-created world. We are not alone in this crazy world; others have similarly distorted versions of reality. These distorted views are so powerfully hypnotic that it seems the world is really like this. We think that's how things are.

It all does seem to make sense and hang together somehow. If it were all completely crazy, we wouldn't have anything in common with others. We can only talk about common experience because underneath all this madness lies the truth of things as they really are. Everyone shares the same basic reality. Built on top of that is an almost equally shared delusion. From a Buddhist perspective, we need to remove the delusion, and these meditations on time and place are excellent ways of doing this. Does anything in our ordinary, confused experience, have real meaning? The answer to that is yes. But don't expect me to say what that is. That would be a very tall order. All I can do is explain why we do these meditations, how they work, and how they can be misunderstood.

It might be tempting to explain the experience of déjà vu in terms of habit patterns, neurons, or something to do with the brain. There is probably also some physiological or neurological explanation that would explain why the past seems to flash before our eyes when we die. Unfortunately, our normal explanations are always made in terms of the confused world. They can't help us escape from our confusion.

To think in this conventional way during a practice session is to effectively abandon the meditation. We will never get outside the circle of our confusion by doing this. Instead, we simply need to rely on whatever presents itself directly to us. Any sense of déjà vu is always a present experience, and the present is completely ungraspable. It's only by working in this way, with our direct experience, that we can get to discover anything genuine.

Hunting the White Hart

Having passed through the collapse of place and time, and having reached the other side, it is no longer necessary to ask where our memories and experiences are stored. It is only at the confused level that we need think in terms of things to be stored and places to store them.

Take an example from physics. Light is a vibration. Sound is also a vibration. Because sound vibrates in air, scientists at one point thought that light must also vibrate in some medium, which they called ether. This idea was later shown to be false—although light is indeed a vibration, it is not a vibration of anything. So even at this ordinary level of understanding we have the idea of vibration without anything vibrating. And when we consider the phenomenon of memory, there's no reason to assume it has to be stored anywhere.

Doing these practices is a bit like hunting, and there is the same kind of challenge involved. I particularly like an image found in fairy stories and other folk tales. A hunter is pursuing a white hart that disappears into a fairy mound; following it, he ends up in a different world. This rather romantic description may not have the frisson of terror that goes with insight, although perhaps it should.

When we practice, it's a bit like trying to catch something by watching the way it moves. As we become lost in memories and take them as real, we keep reminding ourselves that this is a present experience. We focus and press on with a kind of hunting mentality, not with the expectation of insight, but with the wish to catch the moment. Similarly, if we want to discover something about the real nature of anger, we first need to catch the anger at the moment it arises, which brings us happily to our next topic: the wisdom that lies at the heart of negative emotions.

12. Seeing Wisdom in the Emotions

STRONG EMOTIONS tend to cause problems for both ourselves and others, which is why there are so many methods for controlling them. A great deal could be said about the controlling approach, but it's not what we are concerned with here.

In this context we are interested in strong emotions not because they are so troublesome but because they are more obvious. Strong emotions present themselves in a clear and unmistakable fashion. There is some quality of wisdom present within all emotions, however they manifest, but it's much easier to link into this quality when the emotion is strong and clear rather than feeble or diffuse.

Buddhists tend to view the practices based on this approach somewhat nervously, because it can easily sound like we are encouraging the very emotions that produce negative karma. Certainly, if we arouse strong emotions without relating to them properly, we will cause ourselves much bigger problems than we already have. So please be clear that this approach is not about whipping up strong emotions. We have quite enough material of this kind to work with already; and we definitely don't need to create any more. But when strong emotions do arise, this is a way to realize something about their essential nature rather than just another means for controlling them.

Three Basic Types of Negative Emotion

There are three basic types of negative emotions, or *kleshas* as they are called in Sanskrit. One type is associated with hatred and rejection. These kleshas are considered to be the easiest to deal with, strangely enough, because they present themselves in a single, unconfused way.

The second type of klesha is connected with desire and attraction. These emotions are more complicated, with many more nuances. It can sometimes be difficult to know where we are with desire.

The third type of klesha is associated with confusion. These are muddy and muddled in some way. In the West we don't associate confusion with emotion at all, and so confusion is probably the most difficult emotion to see. In some sense it's the strongest emotion we have. It is certainly the most difficult to relate to.

One Neck to Cut

Hatred is thought to be extremely destructive and the cause of our entering into states of misery for a very long time. The hopeful thing about hatred, it is said, is that it is relatively easy to cure. Hatred is very simple. It only has one neck to cut, whereas desire is more complex and many-headed.

The power of hatred is used in radically different ways, depending on whether confusion is present. The general thrust of hatred is to destroy those things we don't like—to remove antagonistic people and situations from our lives. We try to use the natural sharpness and clarity of hatred to overcome problems in conditioned existence, but it inevitably leads us into endless further difficulties.

The wisdom aspect of hatred is concerned with destroying obstacles and removing hindrances to awareness. It is also associated with sharpness and clarity, but in this case the clarity of vision. Unconfused clarity is like a weapon that cuts through anything that hinders our vision. It is sharp in removing confusion and misunderstanding. It lays open the workings of samsara and is associated with awakening, the most positive thing there is. It is a direct experience of the sword of *prajna,* or wisdom, itself.

To connect with the wisdom in hatred, we first have to notice the moment it arises. This is when hatred is strongest. If we can catch that moment, it becomes possible to cut through the hatred. This does not involve rejecting or repressing anything. What is cut is our attachment to hatred. We can then let it go and allow it to dissolve.

We are very strongly attached to our emotions. Negative or positive, our lives become identified with their strength and power. So when we cut through that identification, it becomes a matter of life and death. That is why the imagery of swords and other cutting weapons is often used for this.

Here, There, and Everywhere

With desire, it is more a question of linking into the feeling aspect of experience and then extending this out into other areas. Desire is many-headed, like the hydra, so cutting off its head, as it were, just makes it spring up here, there, and everywhere. Working with desire is more about uniting with the nature of the experience than it is about cutting.

Now linking up with things in this way may sound much more pleasant a thing to do; but in practice, it isn't. While we like to enjoy and savor our pleasures, we also want to be able to stand back from them. It would be all a bit too much to become one with the object of our enjoyment. If we get into any kind of pleasure to the point of identifying with it, the experience is rather terrifying.

Desire is said to be less dangerous than ignorance because it doesn't necessarily send us into really painful circumstances. It might cause us frustration or the misery of unsatisfied longing, but unless we focus on this in an intense way—and involve ourselves in other kinds of negativity as a result—it won't send us into the "lower realms," as traditional Buddhists might say.

Like ignorance, desire is strongly ingrained within us and is therefore difficult to remove. The Buddha's teaching on the origin of suffering says that suffering is due to desire. Ignorance lies behind desire, and it creates the basis for conditioned existence. But the desire for existence and pleasant things—and for avoiding unpleasant things—is the second most powerful driving force there is. If ignorance creates the clockwork of samsara, desire is the key that winds it up and keeps it all going.

Both Dangerous and Difficult

The Mahayana text *Nitartha Vinaya* is concerned with how a bodhisattva should relate to greed, hatred, and ignorance. It talks about ignorance as being the worst of all the negative emotions, because it is the most dangerous to have and the most difficult to get rid of. Ignorance is dangerous because it causes us to drift on the ocean of samsara, where we might get into all kinds of disastrous situations and get shipwrecked at any time. Every unfortunate situation we could ever get into ultimately comes from ignorance. It is difficult to remove because it is so deeply ingrained within us.

Confusion and ignorance are like depression in many ways. When we are depressed, there seems to be no end or edge to it; the whole world is flavored with depression. Similarly, confusion surrounds us like mist or fog. It has an all-pervading and claustrophobic quality. When working with dullness, confusion, or depression, we must endeavor to retain something of the underlying spaciousness, and then let go, or dissolve, the negative feeling that goes with it.

Anger is easier to work with in a practical way because it is so clear cut. Desire is more slippery, and confusion can be difficult to pin down. That's why anger is often the first emotion considered in this kind of training.

13. Working with Anger and Desire

THREE THINGS need to be disentangled whenever we work with any strong emotion, such as anger: the anger, or hatred, itself; the feeling associated with anger; and the action that comes from it.

We all know that anger creates a physical feeling. The feeling is an intermediary, or bridge, between the anger and our angry response. It is not so easy to catch this bodily feeling as it arises. We probably don't notice the feeling until we are already in the midst of an outburst, or even after the event. Often, we go directly from anger to an angry reaction without noticing that it's the feeling that pushes us forward. If we can stay with the feeling without responding, however, we will see how it drives us into action.

In the beginning, we mostly think of hatred only in terms of the actions that spring from it. As we become a little more sophisticated, we see how the feelings lead to the angry response. But is the feeling of anger the same thing as the anger itself? No, there is a moment where we are angry but before that explosion of feeling has happened. The feeling and the emotion only seem to be the same because the two aspects have become so completely identified. It's only by catching the feeling at the moment it arises that we can home in on the distinction.

Ordinarily, when we say we are working with anger, we mean we're either trying to avoid situations that cause anger to arise, or we are looking for ways to ameliorate its effects. This is not the same as having power over anger at the moment it arises, which is something only Buddhists seem to talk about.

We are not talking here about suppressing anger. We are not denying our angry feelings, or trying to crush them because we don't wish to acknowledge their existence. In this practice we allow those feelings some space, but without giving vent to them or letting them push us into action.

There is something very special about catching anger at the moment it arises. We get to see that two things are going on: the pure emotionality of anger and our attachment to it. As we saw in the earlier section on double negativity, the emotion itself isn't particularly problematic, and we don't need to cut that. The problem lies in our attachment to the anger, and the way we become completely absorbed into it. At that moment we are so totally identified with the anger or hatred that it seems to be our very life itself, which is why it's so difficult to give up. It is that complete egocentric identification with the emotion that needs to be cut through.

A *Statement of Intent*

We have to be very determined if we want to catch the feeling of anger at the moment it arises and perform the Dharma action of cutting the aorta of our attachment. For some people, just making a definite wish to do this is enough. For others that wish needs to be elaborated into some statement of intent, a kind of vow to catch the moment.

No matter which method we use, and however strong our intention, we probably won't succeed at first. A situation arises and we get angry, and only as the anger subsides do we think, "Oh damn, I could have caught it earlier, but I didn't remember!" When that happens, we just need to strengthen our resolve to catch it the next time. We may still be a long way off from catching the moment, but at least it's a step in the right direction.

That intention makes it possible to notice the feeling of anger earlier and earlier in the process. In this way you can gradually move toward the point when the anger bursts forth. Once it has, you can turn toward the feeling, without allowing it to push you into action. Internally, you may squirm or feel like striking out, and you may come up with all kinds of justifications for taking action. Whatever arises, don't react; just surrender to the feeling. If you are trembling with rage, stay with the trembling. If you're burning or seething and feel a tremendous pressure to snap at someone, just stay with it.

One difficulty is that we can't really prepare ourselves in advance or predict when somebody or something will trigger us off. Consequently, we need to be aware very quickly. Maybe somebody makes an incredibly annoying and provoking remark, quite out of the blue, or someone's briefcase bangs against you on the train, and bang!—you are in an explosion of rage.

And this happens in an instant—in a snap of the fingers! There are other Dharma methods that use mental imagery, but there is no time for that here. By the time you imagine your sword or some other image, the moment is gone and you've missed your chance. However, it might be useful before the event, as a kind of inspiration. You could associate the intention to catch the moment with some imagery, like the sword of prajna, as way of strengthening your resolve. But in the actual moment, your mind itself has to be the sword.

There is a wonderful simplicity about this approach. If your heart's wish is to catch that moment, and you persist over time, eventually you will succeed.

Too Simple for Justifications

It is possible, but by no means easy, to let go of the anger when it is at its height. Why is it difficult? That single moment epitomizes all the justifications we can have for being angry, and the biggest justification of them all is that the anger is "me." Letting go of our anger at that point is like committing suicide because we are so identified with it.

Anger is a very powerful and energetic emotion, which is why we like it sometimes. Anger is tremendously alive, and in that moment it's as though all our existence is in the anger. We could find infinite reasons to justify our anger, but this is almost beyond conceptual justifications. All our justifications are boiled down into this very simple moment. We could work out the details before and afterward, but on the spot there is just the sense, "this is me!" At that point we either cut through the anger or we don't.

How do we make that choice? At that moment everything within us does not want that to happen. And what's more, we have to cut through our ego-clinging immediately; the window of opportunity is very small.

So what gives us the confidence to perform the action of cutting? It is the *adhisthana*, the inspiration and sustaining power, of our teachers that provides the basis. We can't do it on our own because ego never cuts its own throat; it's not that kind of animal. In this situation, the inspiration to let go—to "die" in this sense—has to come from elsewhere.

By cutting through the sense of self that clings to the anger, not only do we get a clear perception of what Buddhists call "non-self," we also cut through the heart of the double negativity—the concept of self and all those self-justifications—that makes our ordinary anger such a problem. What we are left with is the single negativity, which manifests as a very sharp clarity, and great simplicity of mind.

The Buddhist tantras talk about the transformation of the emotions and seeing their ultimate nature. This all happens in that moment of letting go. Generally speaking, this is only the beginning of the process of transformation, just a flash experience of it. However genuine and truthful those first experiences are, it will be a very long while before the process of seeing—and freeing—the nature of anger is complete.

Staying with the Feeling

Until we can catch that special moment, the focus of the practice is on the feelings produced by our anger. We need to stay with those uncomfortable, almost insufferable feelings, as they rise to a peak and fall away, without allowing them to push us into action.

It's like the approach we take in formless meditation. When strong anger arises we can treat it as a powerful guest. We can relax into it and feel the personality of the guest. We may well seethe and want to lash out at the person who has made us angry. Instead, we stay with the feeling, using it as a kind of meditation object, until eventually it fades away, in the same way everything does.

Generally speaking, this method is only effective with anger that is intense enough to identify as an individual experience: a brief outburst of rage, for example, rather than an ongoing flickering irritability or aggression. Such outbursts can be caused by something someone says, or by the indifference of someone carelessly kicking us or treading on our toes. Any number of such things could trigger it off.

The question is, what happens after that explosion? Do you say something in an angry tone? Do you kick some inanimate object rather than hit the person concerned? Perhaps you just boil inside? Maybe you experience some combination of all three responses, as you continue to justify the anger, until gradually it all fades away.

As our awareness develops, we get the opportunity to open out to those feelings earlier in the process. For example, we can catch ourselves just before making the snappy remark and then stay with the pressure to respond, without giving vent to the anger or free reign to all those negative self-justifications.

We can think of this in terms of mandala principle. If we allow ourselves to be carried away by hatred, the mandala of hatred gets ever bigger and encompasses more and more things. It expands in waves, multiplying out into other areas of our lives.

By meditating in this way, the mandala of hatred becomes smaller, finer, and more precise; smaller in time, because it arises and finishes within a shorter period; and in space, because it no longer leaves the narrow confines of the original cause of the outburst. In that way the mandala of hatred becomes ever smaller.

Other Methods for Handling Anger

There are many other Buddhist methods for handling anger that can be helpful. One approach is that of opposition—whenever you feel angry, you meditate on love and compassion. This counteracts the anger and puts a stop to it.

An alternative method is to see that your anger is empty or that the reason for your anger is nonsensical. A typical argument might go like this: I am angry with an acquaintance. Because I am practicing Dharma, this person has a connection to Dharma through me. Sooner or later, through the power of that Dharma connection, he or she will eventually become a Buddha. Since I wouldn't get angry with a Buddha, why should I get angry with someone who is going to become a Buddha?

Another method is to see how very changeable the mind is. Today you may be very angry with someone and view them as an enemy, but under different circumstances you might find them quite likeable. It may be difficult to envisage that while they're behaving badly toward you. If you use your imagination, however, you can see how you might even become good friends once the situation changes.

Samsara is like a great boiling pot, seething with the activity of karma and continually changing connections and circumstances. One day this enemy will be a friend—maybe later in this life or in a future one, who knows? This being the case, as the great Dilgo Khyentse Rinpoche once said, why not feel friendly toward them *now*?

Another way used to stop anger is to ask yourself what exactly you are angry about? If someone mindlessly steps on your foot, are you angry with their feet, or their navel, or their head? Are you angry with their stream of thoughts or the words that come out of their mouth? Looking at it this way, you can't find any specific thing to be angry with. You might say, "I'm angry with all of it!" But since "all of it" is just a collection of those separate bits, that doesn't make any sense either. This type of argument is used to make us realize that our anger is really a bit stupid.

Whatever method you use, please don't think you need to increase your anger to make it work. We all have quite enough anger already. Nevertheless, if the anger is not sufficiently pronounced, it is difficult to apply the main method I have been describing in this chapter.

The great yogins of this tradition tell us that there is a strong wisdom, a revelatory nature, in the heart of anger. And if we suppress our anger we will never find that out.

The Meaning of Transformation

By cutting through our attachment to hatred, it is transformed, and there is the recognition—and release—of the wisdom that exists within it. Now, we might assume that those who have accomplished this energy of clarity will always appear to be happy, energetic individuals. But it doesn't necessarily work like that. They may even seem to be rather angry people. We have only to look at the life of Marpa, and there are many other examples.

Trungpa Rinpoche said that Vimalamitra would get very angry with people who didn't understand the Dharma. If that were just ordinary rage, caused by their failure to understand, it would be pretty useless. But Vimalamitra's anger affected the people he encountered in a positive way, and he was able to cut through some of their obstructions, turning their minds more deeply toward Dharma. Anger of this kind is always orientated toward overcoming obstacles—either further obstacles within oneself or those that exist within others. It's very different from ordinary anger.

While it is good to talk about the possibility of transforming anger, we need to be very careful not to get carried away by it. Obviously there is always the danger that someone attempts this and ends up getting angry in an ordinary way. Furthermore, it's no good thinking your anger is special because you are a Dharma practitioner and can therefore go around putting other people right—although it can be interesting when two people who think like this meet one another.

Nevertheless, it is indeed possible to transform anger so that it helps others. How do we recognize an individual who can do this? We are unlikely to meet someone who can do this at the highest level. It is more common to find an individual where this ability comes and goes, but even that is rather unusual. Like everything in Dharma training, we need to use our own intuition, our feeling for the person and the effect he or she has on us, to determine whether the anger is useful or not.

When anger is genuinely transformed, it energizes everything you do. If you are talking with a really irritating person, for example, you might find the situation amusing rather than annoying. Or, when a difficult situation is developing, you may be able to say something to resolve it. Your response comes from a kind of clarity that sees the significance in things.

By cutting through the double negativity, the energy of anger is transformed into a different way of experiencing the world.

In order to develop understanding, we need clear-headedness, emotional clarity, and consequently some ordinary sense of control. But the Buddhadharma is not some ancient system of psychotherapy; it is concerned with something totally different. It is more concerned with what emotions are, in and of themselves, and not with anger management.

There is a special quality of wisdom in the heart of our anger and other emotions, which needs to be met face to face. And we need to discover for ourselves just why we don't want to do that.

On Fear

Fear is another important emotion that—although it's not technically a *klesha*—can be treated in a similar way to hatred. Again, there are the three aspects: the moment fear arises; the feeling this produces in us; and the sense of movement, of wanting to flee the situation. These feelings push us into action. As with anger, we identify the fear with the feeling, or even with the action of flight. But, again, it is possible to travel backward along the path that leads to the action—to go back into the feeling of fear, without responding to it.

We don't need to expose ourselves to actual physical danger to do this. As with anger, it's really a matter of common sense. If we're about to be run over by a bus, clearly we need to respond by getting out of the way. If we see someone harming a child, obviously we take immediate action. But if it's only a matter of rudeness, or a petty attack on your ego, does it really matter? This practice is about discovering the real nature of our emotions, and maybe we just need to keep that underlying intention in view.

Wanting and Enjoying

Working with desire is a different matter, although it starts with the same three aspects. First there is the actual desire, the wanting of something or somebody. Then there is a physical feeling: a rush of heat in the body and a sensation almost of wanting to dissolve out toward the object of our desire, to draw it into us and encompass it. And that feeling connects either to some kind of outward physical or verbal response or to a mental explosion of internal desire.

The desire could be for something we don't have or the enjoyment of something we already possess, which amounts to the same thing really. Desire is something we project outward onto another person or object. We think it exists externally, within the object of our desire. But desire actually lies in our own body and mind, which is why we relate to it through the feelings it produces.

Through following this path we become mindful of what it is to enjoy or want something. Could we make the wanting of something into the enjoyment of it? Normally we think that just wanting something is not enough; to enjoy anything we must possess it. But there is a strong affinity between wanting and enjoying. We need to connect with the wanting aspect first, the feelings that go with desire. Then, once we are enjoying something, we can link into the actual feeling of enjoyment.

We need to work with the feelings of both wanting and enjoyment if we are to investigate the subtleties that make the two seem different.

Relaxing into Enjoyment

For most of us, enjoyment is a sense of surfing from peak to peak and ignoring everything in between. It is important to enjoy the whole experience, the way it fluctuates up and down, rather than always to be looking toward the next high spot. By letting the whole experience seep into us, we may find there is more to be discovered in the little "downs" than in the "ups."

Enjoyment tends to be localized, involving the tongue, nose, or some other part of the body. We need to let these feelings grow until we can inhabit or rest in them. At that point, we may well have quite different takes on what occurs in our bodies, which is why there are so many techniques and ways of relating to the body.

Working with desire and enjoyment requires a different approach than hatred. There's not so much the idea of cutting. The basic method involves relaxing into the feeling of enjoyment. By allowing the feeling to grow until it has a quality of spaciousness—instead of being just an isolated feeling—it becomes all-pervading. At that point you can open out and abandon yourself to the feeling. If you were able to catch this completely, you might even become unconscious because the sensation is so intense.

As you move into the feeling, the sense of separateness between you and the feeling lessens. It's like you are dissolving away. And you won't like this at all—with apologies for always coming back to the same point—because it is like dying.

Again, we can think of this in mandala terms. To transform desire, the feeling has to become completely spacious and all-pervading, so that it is no longer confined to a particular person or object. In this sense the mandala of desire expands to encompass everything, in contrast to the mandala of hatred which becomes increasingly small. And just as hatred is transformed into clarity, desire becomes transformed into a kind of universal sensitivity—the great bliss, as it is sometimes called.

Always Rather Scary

The sense of dying is associated symbolically with the loss of ego and the collapse of our world. Any strong sensation of desire or union can cause this kind of dissolution and bring about some experience of non-ego or collapse. This is always rather scary, which is why we usually want our enjoyments to remain external.

We can see this in very simple everyday experiences. For example, we jump when there's a loud noise. Why? Normally we'd say that a sudden loud noise means we are under some sort of threat. But that doesn't necessarily follow, and from a Buddhist point of view it's nonsense. The reason we're frightened by loud noises is because we let ourselves go into the experience. The strength and power of that letting go causes an experience of oneness, and that's what we fear. It's not the noise of a sudden flash-bang that is so frightening, but the fear of non-ego, the fear that we're going to die, or at least the beginning of that process of dissolution. The only reason it doesn't present itself like that is because it all happens so fast.

From ego's point of view, all strong experiences are bad news because they involve the kind of unity that causes both ego and the world to collapse. Ego always wants everything on its own terms. It tries to keep everything at arms length. Ego is threatened by any experience that gets too close, and it makes no difference whether this has to do with hatred, desire, or even pure awareness. All such experiences seem like a betrayal because they move toward a world that ego can't live in.

As we practice by collapsing past, present, and future, or our notion of place, we will experience a real sense of emptiness, a state beyond concepts. This might all sound very high and wonderful and incredibly difficult to accomplish. Surprisingly enough, it is not that difficult. Yes, we need to apply ourselves in a dedicated way. We need the confidence to carry it through, and to let go of any emotional resistance that says, "I don't want to look at this!" That's not so easy to do. But while it is difficult, it's not *that* difficult.

Play, Skill, and Beauty

Tibetans traditionally talk about three things that need be cultivated in Dharma practice. These might be translated as *play, skill,* and *beauty*.

Beauty refers to the rightness of what happens as we exercise the qualities of play and skill in our mind. We can sometimes sense when things are moving in the right way; when we are dealing skillfully and harmoniously with our experience. The beauty aspect is a kind of feedback that confirms this.

Skill includes the idea of power and creativity. It is skill that enables us to catch anger at the moment it arises. And the nearer we get to that point, the greater our skill becomes.

The *play* aspect is the enjoyment involved in our practice. Instead of treating the whole business as a great, heavy, and serious matter, we could treat it more like a game. The way the practice of Dharma works on our minds is something we can enjoy. And we can feel happy about the skill that we gradually acquire.

Thinking of your meditation as something heavy and deadly serious is ego's version of practice. Working with the strong emotions is a considerable matter, there's no doubt about that; but we could lighten up a bit. There is actually a lot of fun and enjoyment involved in learning to handle our emotions. We could take delight in becoming more skilled in catching our hatred as it arises. We could feel happy about training to handle negativity properly; the mere fact of working skillfully with negativity puts a kind of joy into it.

It is all part of the game, and it's a good game at that. The feeling of satisfaction and rightness that goes along with being able to do this is the aesthetic side. That's the beauty of it.

PART 4. THE PURSUIT OF TRUTH

& The Truth of the Path

"If circumstances lead me, I will find
Where truth is hid, though it were hid indeed
Within the centre."
—William Shakespeare, *Hamlet*

*We could say there is a transcendent peace to be found
in the nature of truth, because it is the truth that moves
us to search in the first place, and it is the truth that we
are searching for. Because we only find genuine peace
when we realize truth, the truth is peace.*

14. The Importance of the Path

THE FOURTH NOBLE TRUTH is the path, or *marga* in Sanskrit. Having worked through the first three truths, you might wonder what there is left to accomplish. We have uncovered the problem—which is the focus of the first truth—by experiencing things in a raw and direct way. The second truth brings the realization of just how narrow we become by hanging on to the way we are. The third truth, the cessation of suffering, inspires us to go beyond those conceptual frameworks. It introduces ways to collapse time and space and discover the nature of our emotions. What more could there be? Surely we've reached the end?

Why do we need to follow a path? It's because we won't have done any of this well enough. Despite having done our best to address the first three truths, we won't have plumbed their depths. We may have opened up and gone beyond time and space to some extent. We may have seen something of the true nature of emotions. Nevertheless, it's just a taste of what is possible. There is still an amazingly long way to go.

Through our practice we realize the emptiness of certain key ideas about the universe we live in. These methods allow us to begin letting go of the things we cling to and grasp at. But we have barely started to work directly with the emotions of clinging and grasping. So we still have a very long path to follow, although that's no reason to feel dejected. It's actually very inspiring, provided you think about it in the right way.

Pleasant and Unpleasant

It is interesting to see just how effective and disturbing these practices are. The collapse of past, present, and future is disturbing, to put it mildly. But what does that show us? It shows that while we have been very effective in removing the object of grasping, we haven't removed the grasping itself.

This is a crucial aspect of the fourth truth, the truth of the path. It takes a long time to remove the clinging and grasping: our wanting and needing for things to be solid, graspable, and always within our power or compass. When we realize that nothing in our experience is like that, we wake up to a world in which the old values and ways of thinking don't obtain any more. This doesn't stop us hankering after them, however, and that makes us feel very disturbed.

It's as if we have been asleep all our lives, and suddenly we wake up to our first experience of reality, which is the nonexistence and invalidity of all those deeply held notions. This undermines our egocentric ambition and self-clinging. It undercuts our sense of being the source of everything and the center of the universe. And it is like nothing we have ever experienced. In fact, it's more like a tremendously potent vision than any kind of experience we could imagine; it's a completely different way of viewing the world.

Something within us doesn't want to see that truth. There is a kind of horror in the realization that we've been wrong from the very beginning and need to start all over again. At that point most of us are unable to look beyond the experience of emptiness and see what is really there. Nevertheless, the first time this happens is a tremendous watershed in one's life—or lives—a complete turning around in our experience, and a huge step forward.

When we talk about people being enlightened, generally speaking it's this first step that is meant. It takes much longer to see what lies beyond that false vision; to see what is real. The full awakening of a Buddha, such as Shakyamuni, requires the completion of both steps. We cannot realize the truth in our experience without first seeing the emptiness of what is false. It's not possible to jump straight from the beginning to the end, and avoid the unpleasant bit in the middle; insight doesn't seem to work like that.

Actually, this realization is both pleasant and unpleasant. It's a great relief to realize there is a truth to discover that goes beyond anything we thought possible. But however wonderful it may be, it also shakes us up in a most disturbing way. That is why enlightenment isn't easy. In some ways enlightenment should be obvious. It's just a question of seeing what is there before us. How could we avoid doing that? Well, our wrongheaded clinging to false notions prevents us from seeing things as they are.

Undoing that clinging is both painful and wonderful at the same time. It's such a powerful habit that any one experience of the true nature of things—no matter how vast or deep—can't change it. The emotions of clinging and grasping are tremendously difficult to shift, so even once we've had some genuine vision, it takes a very long time to mature into it.

I think it was the great Buddhist logician Dignaga who said that it's much more difficult to understand the real nature of the phenomenal world around us than it is to realize emptiness. Buddhists tend to think that emptiness is incredibly subtle and difficult to understand and realize. Dignaga taught that while emptiness is indeed very subtle, only buddhas can understand the real nature of phenomena.

Waving the Flag

New students sometimes ask me why they need to bother with sitting meditation. They would be much happier meditating as they walk about during the day. Couldn't they just practice in everyday life? How wonderful it would be if we could do that. Unfortunately, it is the most difficult practice of all. It's undoubtedly easier to get our first inspiration and connection through sitting meditation. We can then go on to practice in everyday life. But we would be very foolish to try to replace one with the other.

The tradition maintains that we all need to meditate in formal sessions until we are far along the path. Only at that point, when everything we experience feeds into our insight, is sitting practice no longer necessary.

But even then, we need to set an example, and wave the flag of meditation for others. Otherwise people will say, "Well, he never meditates so why should we?"

You don't have to think of it as the Buddhist chore! Even when it's no longer strictly necessary, meditation can be enjoyable and relaxing; and we all need to rest. Once you get more deeply into meditation, you may well find great enjoyment in just sitting. It's not so terrible really.

As Bad as the End of the World

Ultimately, our task, as Buddhist practitioners, is to see the nature of the universe of all possible experience. That sounds very grand, but we have to start by gaining some deeper realization of where we are now, and then expand or open out beyond that. This process takes a very long time. In Mahayana Buddhism, it is sometimes said to take "three incalculable *kalpas*," which is an astronomical number of years. So what could that possibly mean, when we've just talked about collapsing space and time?

Even after the three times have collapsed, it seems there is still the feeling of duration, and we can play between the two. If we encounter the vastness of space and time as a direct experience, it won't be in terms of past, present, and future, but as an ungraspable vision, beyond anything we can describe.

The practices described in part 3 are mostly focused on removing the object of grasping by undermining the way we view the world. Our biggest job, however, is to work with that fundamental emotional grasping itself: that grasping at things as real, and grasping at some solid ground to stand on.

For most of us, the ordinary world that we cling to is real, solid, and graspable. Through practicing these meditations the world as we know it seems to fall apart, but the craving and grasping continues. Shockingly, the world seems to collapse around us. But how can that be? It can't collapse, just like that. We are simply seeing the world as it really is, and it's shocking to see that the objects of our grasping are truly ungraspable.

The first thing we notice, at this point, is a sense of loss. The mind and heart that grasps has lost everything it loves and can't see anything beyond that. We are like a frightened child whose toy has been taken away. Trungpa Rinpoche once said, "Don't cry! It's not as bad as that!" Well it seems that bad. It feels like the end of the world. Now, it could be argued that nothing has been lost, because the grasped-at world is like a bad dream, but we remain very attached to that dream, and dearly want for it to be real.

Traditional texts sometimes talk about special powers, such as the ability to walk through walls. Why can't we do such things? One reason is because of our great attachment to the universe as a solid, reliable place where people can't walk through walls.

We are very attached to this world and the way it seems to operate. We might fantasize about how to "do amazing things and astonish your friends," as it said on my childhood box of magic tricks. But we wouldn't really like the world to be as fluid as that. To continue existing in the old familiar way we need a stable backdrop. And we don't want that backdrop to suddenly develop holes and strange quirks—even if we are making them ourselves—which is why we stay with our pain.

Most of us might well prefer a familiar pain to an unfamiliar kind of bliss. Bliss would be okay if it fits into our ordinary framework of experience; otherwise, we may prefer the pain. If I have toothache, at least it proves I have teeth. It is sad to think this could be the reason for many more significant limitations than just the inability to walk through walls.

Why isn't it easy to become enlightened? If everything is so direct, surely we ought to become enlightened in an instant—just like that! But we don't, because ego is afraid it will disappear. The apparent solidity of our world, with all its pains and irritations, serves to confirm our existence. And, from ego's point of view, that is more important than anything else.

Karmic Vision

Our ordinary way of viewing the world is sometimes described as a *karmic vision*. We see things a certain way because of our particular bodily set-up and the conditioning of past actions.

These two factors connect us with other beings with a similar set-up, which is how we come to live and work together in a particular world of experience. Other creatures may seem very dissimilar, but in some ways they aren't that different from us. Cats, for example, may not be able to become awakened, but their physical set-up connects them with us in ways that allow them to appear in our world and make good pets!

There is a connection between the human and animal worlds that extends to include certain classes of nonhuman beings, beings that most people don't even believe in any more. We don't need to consider those nonhuman beings here, beyond keeping an open mind about their existence. The point is that all beings share a certain similarity of vision. And, the more alike they are, the more sense of community there is. Two human beings, for example, would have a greater sense of shared world than a human being and a lizard; nevertheless, there is still some kind of connection there.

In some sense, all our perceptions, thoughts, and concepts are distorted, one-sided versions of some deeper reality. In the most profound Dharma teachings, even the senses and sense objects—as we think of them—are viewed as "unnecessary complications of existence." We can get closer to reality than that. We could reach a direct understanding of truth that passes beyond our karmic vision of the world.

A Springboard Toward the Truth

When awakened beings appear in the world, it seems as if they have a body and physiological set-up similar to our own. They use the same kind of language we do, they talk about themselves and about such things as past, present, and future. But this doesn't mean they subscribe to these notions. Awakened ones appear in this way for our benefit, not for their own. And if you were to ask them what the universe is really like, they would probably tell you to become enlightened and see for yourself.

What is the point of the universe? Why does anything exist at all? Such questions can't be answered in conceptual terms. Any answer is at the level of a direct understanding of truth, which goes beyond our conceptual or karmic vision of the world. We can experience gaps in this vision—and flashes of insight into something deeper—through our meditation practice. As we proceed along the path, these insights increase until eventually we become great bodhisattvas and, finally, buddhas.

The universe has a structure that accords with wisdom and *vidya*, the direct knowing of things as they truly are. However, no person can impart this direct understanding to another in conceptual terms. While they might produce a description that is especially useful for a certain time and place, it would never be complete.

Buddhist teachers always try to move us toward awakening and away from fixation on the complications of existence. The real answers are never conceptual. Nobody can tell you, "Reality is like this!" or "Read my book for a complete explanation of all the secrets of the universe." The truth has to be perceived directly, which is why even buddhas can never really communicate it to others. It isn't that they don't want to; we just don't have the wherewithal to understand what they are saying. And it isn't a question of intelligence; we simply can't activate this direct seeing in ourselves. So teachers wisely don't attempt the impossible. Instead, they try to arouse this capacity in others, which is what the Buddhist path is all about.

One of the greatest Indian Buddhist masters, certainly for Tibetans, was Guru Rinpoche, the "Lotus Born." He is thought of as being totally enlightened, in a primordial way. But even the greatest gurus must receive teaching, otherwise there is no path to follow. So, in order to demonstrate this truth, one of Guru Rinpoche's life stories tells how he went for instruction to the great teacher Shri Singha, the "Glorious Lion."

Shri Singha gave instruction on the nature of mind to Guru Rinpoche, who meditated and realized this teaching. Shri Singha then called his realization "beyond words and thought, beyond action, beyond anything that can be described." He then said to Guru Rinpoche: "You may be the greatest guru of them all, the very essence of buddhahood. But that will make no difference; you still won't be able to describe this to anyone else!" And it seems the Lotus-Born Guru agreed.

All practitioners find themselves in this situation. Even the greatest buddhas and most accomplished bodhisattvas find it impossible to transmit the nature of mind and being in words. Words can inspire us and act as a vital pointer or a springboard toward the truth. But they can't explain what it's like to leap from the diving board, up into the air, and land in the water. All we can say is, "Come on in, the water is fine!" and encourage other people to venture onto the diving board.

15. Awakened Activity

THESE DAYS, many people feel estranged from the universe around them. The more we learn about the universe through science, the less significant seems the place of human beings within it. Human beings are so dwarfed by the vastness of the stars and galaxies, and the extent of time and space, that anything we do seems quite insignificant.

Now even if this is just an intellectual view, it probably has a negative effect when you apply it to your own experience. As Buddhists, we train to feel confident that we are part of the universe, however vast in time and space it may be. And through our Dharma practice we can begin to realize that the power and potential qualities of every individual person are on a similar scale.

So just as there is cosmic space and time, in Buddhist terms everyone has cosmic qualities, although these are normally hidden. We don't think of ourselves and others as being of much account simply because we never look below the surface.

The truth we are seeking lies within ourselves already, waiting to be revealed. It is also to be found all around us. So in some sense the truth comes to us from without and within at the same time. The truth that seems to swoop down from outside is no different to the truth that wells up within us. They are fundamentally the same.

In Mahayana Buddhism the truth is often talked about in terms of *bodhichitta,* the awakened heart and mind. Bodhichitta is not only about wisdom and insight. It is also about the heart qualities of love, compassion, joy, and the balance of heart and mind needed to see and feel things properly. Without that balance of mind our activity becomes one-sided and partial, and compassion easily turns into sentimentality. In bodhichitta the truth from outside and the truth from inside come together, with truly compassionate activity arising as the play between the two.

The truth also relates to the four kinds of awakened activity, or *four karmas,* as they are called. Karma here has nothing to do with the idea of cause and result; the four karmas are the activities of awakened beings.

The first karma has to do with peace. The truth has a satisfying quality. We feel there is something to be discovered, but don't know what it is, which is very unsatisfactory. It's only by discovering the truth that we become truly at ease and at peace with the world. There is no one ordinary word that covers this. Perhaps we could say there is a transcendent peace to be found in the nature of truth, because it is the truth that moves us to search in the first place, and it is the truth that we are searching for. Because we only find genuine peace when we realize truth, the truth is peace.

Some people don't like the idea of peace; it doesn't sound much fun. But being at peace doesn't mean being passive or collapsing in a great heap. It means we are freed from all the niggling doubts, difficulties, and abrasiveness that arise when we don't connect with life in a truthful way. Nor is peace inactive. It contains all the power and energy associated with compassionate action—but without that constant need for fulfillment.

The second karma is enrichment. The truth enriches because it contains everything we are looking for. All the things we truly long for aren't to be found out there in the world, as they seem to be; they are contained in the truth itself. Because the truth pervades everything, by connecting to it, everything is given to us. We will no longer need to grasp so frenetically at our possessions and personal qualities. Instead, we can take a more carefree attitude, and use them properly, as we never could before. So the truth is enriching and leads to complete fulfillment.

The third karma is seduction. Having once connected to the truth, we can never give it up, and it will never leave us alone. We may wish to abandon the truth, and live our lives without being bothered with it, but we will never succeed. The truth has its own "gravity field," which pulls us in. Since we can't get away from it, we may as well pursue the truth; if we don't, the truth will pursue us!

Truth is also said to be like a lover. We could relate to the truth as we might relate to another man or woman. It is the ultimate love object, could we but see it. The truth might sound too formless to make a good lover, but remember that it permeates the entire physical world, including not only other people and actual lovers, but also all the physical, intellectual, and emotional situations we are connected with. These can become objects of our love as well. And in a strange way they reciprocate, as if we were lovers for them.

Trungpa Rinpoche used to say that the Dharma—which is the same as truth in this context—is "alive from its own side." The Dharma is not something remote and wonderful that we need travel vast distances to discover. The truth, again, if we could but see it, is all around us, and has a kind of activity or movement from its own side. The Dharma has a living quality, which is why it can come to us as a partner, as lover or loved one, in all our enterprises.

The fourth karma is destructive action. The truth has a wrathful face for us. As it wells up in us, we realize the wrong-headedness of all those fundamental notions, such as time and space. Nevertheless, we are still very attached to them. Consequently it's quite frightening when they start to collapse. This destructive aspect of truth comes to us in an almost deathlike, or wrathful, fashion because it removes anything and everything we wrongly cherish.

16. A Mysterious Strength

I F WE WANT to follow the Mahayana, the "great way" of the bodhisattva, we need to develop two kinds of accumulation. The first has been discussed in previous chapters: this is the accumulation of insight, or *jnanasambhara*, through which we see the empty nature of the things we cling to and grasp at. The second is *punyasambhara*, the accumulation of *punya*, or power.

The Power of Punya

Punya is a difficult word to translate. Basically, it means something like power or influence. It is a somewhat mysterious strength that can accomplish many things. Punya is a force that can be used to change the set of our mind and emotions, the way we feel about the world. Punya may be directed by our intention, or wish. We need the power of punya to transform our emotions and to move the grasping, clinging mind away from self-centeredness.

Punya comes from the heart intention associated with our actions in the world. Working directly to benefit other people can develop punya. It can also come from creating an inspiring artistic expression of Dharma, something that represents wisdom and compassion. A temple that inspires people to practice, for example, is a kind of physical poetry that manifests Dharma in the world. The actual word of Dharma can also inspire people and creates punya. In Buddhist cultures special copies of Dharma texts are created, a bit like illuminated manuscripts, and they are sometimes carved in stone. When the words of Dharma are recreated in rich and inspiring ways, they become objects of devotion.

This kind of thing has generally acquired a bad name in the West. Some people connect it with empty ritual and the creation of something hollow, like putting money into a church instead of helping the poor. But that misses the point really. Performing actions that are socially valuable and help others does create that power and influence within us; but so does the creation of things that lead and inspire people toward the Dharma. So we need to have both.

Having developed punya, we then need to associate it with an intention of some kind. This is often verbalized as a kind of vow, although intention is perhaps a better way of putting it. The Buddhist word for this is *pranidhana* in Sanskrit, or *mönlam* in Tibetan, and it's a very important notion in Mahayana Buddhism. At the end of a meditation session, for example, we might dedicate everything we've done in order to realize enlightenment for the benefit of others. Doing this affects the emotional flavor that arises as insight begins to develop. It helps us feel at home in the insight, rather than at odds with it. If we don't balance our increasing insight with more and more punya, in the end we will just freak out and go crazy.

We need a really strong weight to settle us stably within the mandala of Dharma, even though we don't yet understand it completely. The power of punya keeps us centered in the Dharma, and because we are seated in the right place, as it were, we won't be too disturbed as our understanding develops and deepens.

The Presence of the Buddha

In the beginning stages of practice, awakening is always presented as something external. At a later stage it may become meaningful to talk about awakening as something within us, but if we do this too early, the whole notion of awakening becomes a fantasy. That's why it is important to begin by thinking of awakening as something outside ourselves. A simple Buddha image can be a good starting point for doing this.

The Buddhist way began 2,500 years ago with Buddha Shakyamuni. We don't really know what he looked like, but the traditional representations provide a good basis for inspiration. Many Buddhist practitioners have images of the Buddha in their homes. In the West, however, beginning practitioners sometimes feel a bit embarrassed about this. They wonder if representations of the Buddha are kept out of sentiment, and notions about graven images may float through their minds. Because of that background, it is important to understand why such images are used, and how we should relate to them.

There isn't much value in having a Buddha image if you think of it as just a bit of metal or wood, sitting in the corner of your meditation room. A Buddha image acts as a physical support for the sense of presence of the Buddha; just as when we meet someone, their physical appearance is a support for their presence. We can get an impression of someone's personality from the way they speak, gesture, and move. But if we reflect on what that person is, we realize they are much more than just their physical appearance and gestures. In a similar fashion, the Buddha image is a visual clue to a sense of presence, in this case the presence of enlightenment.

What do we really know about enlightenment? What could it possibly mean to say that the Buddha is present in the room? One approach is to think of the Buddha as someone who could grant your heart's deepest wish by answering all those fundamental questions about life and meaning.

According to the Buddhadharma, we can only experience those answers as a direct face-to-face realization, at the level of intuition or inspiration (but without the sense of wooliness those words might suggest). A buddha—which literally means "awakened one"—has attained this realization and can transmit it to others. However, this transmission isn't necessarily done through words; it could happen directly, mind to mind; so we don't need a talking Buddha image.

So whenever we enter our meditation room, we come into the presence of the awakened one, someone who could awaken us as well.

A Meeting of Minds

As you walk through the door, try to imagine what it would be like to be in the presence of a Buddha. But don't think about it too hard, as that would be unhelpful. The important thing is to feel what it would be like to be in the presence of an awakened person.

In the Buddhist tradition, we open ourselves out to the presence of the awakened ones through body, speech, and mind. We surrender to them by making physical prostrations, offering ourselves bodily without holding back. We offer ourselves through speech as we recite the words of the refuge formula and the bodhisattva vow; or as we recite poetry and songs that inspire us to feel the awesome nature of an encounter with a truly awakened one. And finally, we rest our minds in that experience.

Sometimes physical offerings are made, such as flowers, incense, lighted candles, and so on. Tibetans traditionally offer seven bowls of water to represent the seven things offered to an honored guest in India. But the details don't matter; the important thing is the simplicity and purity of the offering. Having made our offering, we can then sit in front of the Buddha image and rest our minds, allowing ourselves to come into a kind of communion with the experience of awakening.

This isn't done through some kind of analysis. It works because we are sufficiently awake ourselves, simply because we are human beings following the path, and that's enough to make the connection. It's like the meeting of two minds: one's own mind and some quality of awakened mind. Buddha images are very useful as a focus for that sense of the presence of awakening.

Punya and Devotion

Relating to the presence of the Buddha in this way produces punya, and we can focus the resulting power and influence in the direction of awakening. We can dedicate the punya with the wish that we may become awakened ourselves, in order to help others do the same.

This kind of practice doesn't necessarily develop any great insight. It does, however, connect us to the Buddha's awakening and compassion in a rather mysterious way, based on the fact that we are already connected to enlightenment, whether we like it or not. Even if we are totally unenlightened, we are still connected to awakening because of our intrinsic buddha nature.

The development of insight is one important way to connect with enlightenment. Another way is to develop punya by working with this kind of emotionally focused Dharma. As practitioners, we need to use both approaches.

I don't generally introduce the idea of punya and devotion at the beginning because, in the Western world, we mostly associate devotion and open emotionality with Christianity. Consequently, many practitioners don't want anything to do with it, which is somewhat like throwing the baby out with the bathwater. Conversely, in the Tibetan context, practitioners are usually introduced to devotionally focused practice right at the start, because it's thought to be easier than the process of developing insight.

In fact, the Buddhist approach to devotion is not really the same as in other religions such as Christianity; although it does make use of the same basic emotionality. This only works, however, if we have a proper connection with it, which is natural enough in traditional Buddhist cultures but more problematic in the West.

Nothing Is Left Out

Practicing in the way just described is just sticking your big toe in the water; the process has to go much further, but this first step gives you a flavor of how to proceed. At some point you need to mix this kind of practice with insight.

One way to do this is to learn how to wait in the presence of the Buddha. Having made a gesture with your body, and offered flowers, incense, and inspiring words, you could then rest your mind in a sense of the presence of the Buddha. By simply resting your mind and allowing yourself to wait, insight might arise spontaneously—as if it didn't come from you.

This is an experience of the "Buddha turning the wheel of the Dharma." By focusing the mind and then waiting, we are making a request for the teaching to emerge, and should something come to us, it will seem to come from outside.

Having started down this line, we can extend it in various ways. Material images are always useful because we can relate to them while we go about our everyday activities. However, the Buddha doesn't have to appear as an external image. The Buddha could appear as a figure in our minds, but not as something "visualized" in a heavy-handed way. It could just be a sense of presence, evoked by a simple description of his appearance and qualities.

And why stop at one buddha? Since enlightenment pervades everywhere, you could think of myriad buddhas radiating through the whole of space, all appearing immediately before you—and not just you. Why should you be the only one to have that connection? What about the people you love, don't they need it as well? And don't the people you hate need it even more? Come to that, why not all beings?

You can think that a vast assembly of buddhas, radiating throughout space, is seated before you, while all around you are the friends, relations, and others you love: your parents, children, teachers, and neighbors. All human and nonhuman beings, even cats and other pets—but don't overdo this—are included.

Thinking like this increases our sense of vastness. Nothing is left out: all of enlightenment is in front of us, and every possible kind of being is gathered around us. At this point, we can think that all beings together make physical offerings and repeat the words of refuge or sing songs praising the buddhas and enlightenment.

Finally, all the imagery dissolves away, but the sense of presence remains, and we can rest in this. By working with form in this way, we produce more punya and move toward insight at the same time.

17. Power and Insight

EVENTUALLY we find that punya and insight—power and sig-nificance—like form and formlessness, all feed into each other, because they are not really separate. We start by developing the form. As the form fades away, insight arises. That insight increases and intensifies over time because we have developed punya. The power of the punya also influences the way our emotions are directed, so that we are less disturbed by the emerging insight. Insight, in turn, provides a good basis for punya, by connecting us to what the form is really about.

Form and Formless Practice

The form and formless practices in the Tibetan tantric tradition are called *kyerim* and *dzogrim*, although those two aspects are actually relevant to all Dharma training. The *kye* in kyerim means "form," and *rim* means something like "stage." So roughly speaking, kyerim means "form stage." The *dzog* in dzogrim means "to perfect," or "perfected." This is often translated as "perfection stage," but it really refers to the formless aspect. For our purposes here, we could gloss *kyerim* to mean "form" and *dzog-rim* to mean "formless," although in other contexts they have more specific meanings.

Let's go back to the idea of having all the buddhas before us, with all

sentient beings gathered around. It doesn't really matter whether the buddhas are thought of in a more or less detailed fashion. I don't want to put
too much weight on the detail, because that isn't necessary; it may even
be unhelpful. As you get into the practice, the different forms and appearances may well come to you fairly clearly, in a somewhat spontaneous
fashion. But even if this does occur, the most important thing is the sense
of presence.

Similarly for sentient beings. You just have to get an impression of the
many different kinds of beings, with their varied appearances, personalities, and emotional flavors. You can have a quite light-handed connection to all this, it doesn't have to be hard work.

The purpose of having myriad buddhas at every point in space is to
realize that awakening comes from everywhere. It is not just sloshing
around in space, a bit stronger here, a little weaker over there. We need
a vivid sense of awakening coming from everywhere.

Again, it's no good thinking of sentient beings in too vague a way. We
need just enough form to get a feeling for their separate personalities
extending into space. If we then do the practice of going for refuge, the
sense of devotion could become very strong, as we think of all the beings
around us taking refuge together. Going further, we might think that all
these beings are inspired to become buddhas themselves, so as to be able
to help others. And as they take this vow, all the buddhas before them
witness that commitment.

Another way to connect to enlightenment is by making offerings of
everything you possess, as well as everything of beauty and value in the
world. Accompanied by all sentient beings, you offer all your sense perceptions and every imaginable kind of flower, music, art, and painting; all
the sunsets, sounds, smells, and tastes; anything created by the mind or
hand that seems worthy of offering. All of this is offered to the buddhas
for the sake of complete enlightenment.

The form helps to establish a sense of the presence of awakening, and
a strong experience of going for refuge, taking the bodhisattva vow, or
making offerings. We can then let go of the form and focus more on the
feeling that goes along with taking refuge, arousing bodhichitta, or whatever Dharma activity we are performing. And in the end, everything fades

into a vivid sense of formlessness, which is not vagueness, but a kind of clarity beyond appearances. Finally, we rest the mind without concepts— or as near to that as we can.

By doing this kind of practice regularly and with a light touch, we become completely familiar with what's involved, but without becoming bored. The form may then develop spontaneously and become increasingly vivid, until at some point it seems to be getting in the way.

As the sense of refuge, bodhisattva vow, or offering becomes stronger, the form becomes less and less necessary and gradually fades. Eventually, we can link directly into those experiences in a completely formless way. We could have a formless devotion to refuge, a formless development of bodhichitta, a formless sense of offering, and so on. What's more, they become even more powerful, not less so; it's as if they had been restricted by the form. But we can't approach this powerful level of genuine formlessness without first working extensively with form.

Further along the path, there are many more elaborate practices that combine form and formlessness, insight and punya. There is, for example a very detailed meditation in which we make an offering of our own body. Letting go of attachment to the body is a major accomplishment, and some practitioners spend much of their lives training in this way. This practice not only changes the way we think about our bodies; one side effect is to undermine our attachment to the outside world. As the one begins to collapse, the other goes as well, and a very different vision of the world arises.

The World of Mantra

One of the central practices in both Mahayana Buddhism and Buddhist tantra is the reciting of mantras. A mantra is a kind of formula, a set of syllables that can be repeated in various ways. Each mantra is connected not only to a specific manifestation of enlightenment, but also to the whole milieu and way of viewing the world that goes along with a particular bodhisattva or buddha.

Take, for example, Avalokiteshvara, the great bodhisattva of compassion. A bodhisattva at this level has reached a very high level of realization, virtually indistinguishable from that of a buddha. It is said that Avalokiteshvara has reached the highest level of wisdom, but chooses to remain in the world to help confused sentient beings. So the most important feature of Avalokiteshvara is a tremendous focus on compassion. He expresses the compassionate aspect of awakening.

Avalokiteshvara is often represented in front of an enormous white moon, the moon of compassion, or bodhichitta. Through repetition of his mantra, *om mani padme hum*—perhaps the best known of all mantras—it is thought that we can attune ourselves with the essence of Avalokiteshvara and enter into his world.

The great female bodhisattva Tara also has her own mantra and world, or milieu. Her color is green, representing compassionate activity. All the great bodhisattvas, like Avalokiteshvara and Tara, were once people like ourselves, but through the power of Dharma practice, they became transformed into great beings with the power to help others. It is sometimes asserted that beings at the highest levels of realization have to be male. Tara took a vow to remain a female practitioner throughout all her lives, until she became a great female bodhisattva. By repeating her mantra, we can attune ourselves to Tara and enter her world.

All the great bodhisattvas possess enormous wisdom, compassion, and power, but each one emphasizes one special quality. Vajrapani, for instance, represents the power and energy of awakening. He is blue in color, like a thunderstorm, and has the power to destroy any obstruction. His name means "Vajra-in-Hand," the vajra symbolizing the particular power he represents, which is different in flavor to the compassionate activity of the previous two bodhisattvas.

Another example is Manjushri, who is represented as a sixteen-year-old youth carrying the sword of wisdom and a book. He is especially connected with wisdom and, again, we can enter his milieu by repeating his mantra.

Generally speaking, it isn't sufficient to make just a few repetitions of a mantra. We may well need to repeat it thousands, hundreds of thousands, or even millions of times. Obviously, we should know the meaning of the mantra and its individual syllables. But we also need to know something about the mantra's background—the personification of awakening and world of enlightenment associated with it. For mantra repetition to be really effective, we have to feel a strong connection to that bodhisattva or buddha, and a longing to attune ourselves with his or her world.

There are three aspects involved in mantra-recitation practice, two of which we have already considered—we must know about the background to the mantra, and we must repeat it frequently—but we also need to get some sense of its emptiness. It is sometimes said that mantras should be repeated in a light fashion, so that we see something of the emptiness of the mantra as we recite it. If we do all this sufficiently, at some point the mantra will take off by itself, and become significant in a way that is difficult to describe. That significance is contained within the mantra itself, but it doesn't appear at the beginning, only emerging gradually through the practice.

Practitioners use a string of beads called a *mala* to count mantras. Some mantras are associated with a particular type of bead: most commonly sandalwood, crystal, bone, or bodhichitta seed. There is also significance in the way we touch the mala while reciting the mantra and the way we use our hands, which relates to the idea of *mudra*. Body, voice, and mind are joined as one in the practice of mantra.

The manner of recitation, while not so significant in the beginning, becomes important later on. A mantra might be recited in a longing, devotional fashion, as though there were tears in your eyes. It could be repeated in a rather energetic, angry way. Or with a kind of curiosity, as if you were looking for something in the mantra as you repeat it; as though it were a little world or tiny ball held up to the light. Maybe whatever is inside can only emerge when you view, or feel, the mantra in that way. Another approach would be to repeat the mantra as if you were drunk! This could be quite significant, and you may feel more at home with the mantra after repeating it like that.

Each style of recitation gives the mantra a particular "spin." We might well ask, "What is the point of all this?" Basically it is all to do with form and the way we use the form to connect to the more powerful formless stage.

The mantra is a kind of form. The emotions you feel, and the gestures you make with your fingers as you move the beads, are different kinds of form. The mala itself, and all the different varieties of mala used in various contexts, are a type of form. Even the way you breathe while reciting is a form.

We are using the form to gain some penetrating insight, to get a glimpse of the awakened qualities that lie within the mantra. By reciting a mantra with a sense of longing, it's as if we're saying, "I want to know who you are! I want to be one with you!" Whereas reciting a mantra as though we were drunk or blissed out could lead to a sense of oneness, but without the longing. Or by reciting a mantra with curiosity, some quality of wisdom might be revealed.

There is a tremendous amount, a whole world of understanding, involved in learning about mantra, and mantra repetition. Done properly, and focused in the right way, mantra practice can bring us quite close to the flavor of enlightenment. Obviously this could all go horribly wrong and become just another samsaric trip, which is why we need some basis in insight. Traditionally, the mantra is taught separately in order to simplify matters. But if you want to practice as a yogin or yogini, you must learn how to unify all these different aspects of practice. Then, when your experience begins to open out in an insightful way, you are already connected with that awakened world, and consequently it comes as less of a shock.

By joining insight with compassion and bodhichitta, your practice will become much vaster than it ever could with an ordinary, samsaric, orientation.

18. Transforming the Body

THE GOAL of Mahayana Buddhism is to realize enlightenment for the sake of all sentient beings throughout the universe, a universe that is fantastically extensive, and even vaster than that described in modern cosmology.

As beginner bodhisattvas we practice to develop both insight and punya. Our increasing punya helps to ensure that we aren't shattered by the insight as it unfolds. This is wonderful, but is it enough? The answer is no. We are still on the *marga*, the path of the fourth truth, and at this point we enter a rather strange area of the tradition. This is the idea that our bodies need to be transformed. Why? Because they limit our capacity to generate punya.

We simply can't produce enough punya as we are now. However, it's not really a question of resolving, "I'd better start transforming my body!" As our insight develops, the realization that it's genuinely possible to transform our bodies just arises naturally. And by using methods that follow on from the practices described above, we can go on to generate vast amounts of punya, and then deeper and still further insight, because the two are so closely intertwined.

Back to the Beginning

We can get some sense of why this transformation is necessary by going back to the beginning, to that most basic instruction of openness. If we experience everything as completely as possible, things inevitably become more poignant and precise, and the sensitivity of our mind and body can't help but increase.

We don't usually think of our moment-to-moment experience as anything special. Things don't appear to change very much. Going from one room to another may give us a different sense of space, but most things still look the same. A door that is yellow this morning will be yellow this evening or next week. This apparent continuity fools us into a sense of ongoing identity. If we follow it through, however, we quickly realize that this kind of thinking makes no sense.

In fact everything changes; nothing remains the same, not even the yellow door. Doors are only yellow because of the crudeness of our perception and the yellow label we attach to them. Looking more closely we see that the color is dynamic and changes from moment to moment; and our sense of place is equally dynamic. If we could experience this continuously, we would see that every moment—as it arises—is unique; and every moment disappears, as if it had never existed, only to be followed immediately by another, equally unique, experience.

Too Much to Swallow?

If we experience the continual birth and death of each moment, everything is seen to be new and fresh, from instant to instant. Even a glimpse of this undermines our autopilot and our ability to ignore most of the universe. Everything becomes fresh, vivid, and astonishing. And because each new experience dies from moment to moment, never to arise again, there is also something poignant about this. There is something dear and tender about each and every instant.

Trungpa Rinpoche used a number of images for this experience, all of them rather uncomfortable. He said it was like the rawness of having your skin taken off, so there was no protective barrier between you and your experience. Another was the idea of hot and cold jets of water playing on you simultaneously. He finished by calling the whole experience "as delightful as swallowing a baby porcupine"! Can you imagine anything less delightful than swallowing a baby porcupine? The world comes to us with a tremendous vividness and sharpness, right into our most sensitive part, an experience we couldn't survive as we are now. Our ordinary physical and emotional set-up can't encompass such intensity, and we would die instantly if we suddenly became that open, sensitive, and aware.

That's why our bodies have to be transformed. However, this doesn't mean the body pops like a bubble, as it miraculously changes into some other form. Any transformation is from "our side," as it were; to others we might appear much the same. Other people have their own view of things, and they won't necessarily see any change, unless they have a strong connection with us already.

There are many stories about yogins, gurus, and siddhas who have gone through this transformation, but it's usually only perceived by those very close to them, and never by everyone. When great bodhisattvas pass away and arise again out of compassion for others, they appear in seemingly ordinary bodies; but from their perspective, it's a quite different matter.

Buddhist Yoga

As I mentioned above, this tradition starts with formless meditation, working directly with the flow of thoughts and feelings, and from that basis we move on to develop various other ways of generating insight and punya. Only later does it become appropriate to introduce the less-publicized methods of Buddhist yoga, which make much greater use of the body.

Here in the West, Hindu hatha yoga has the highest profile and is often practiced without much introduction. Buddhist physical yoga is generally taught much later on the path, after students have practiced extensively in other ways to develop the mind and heart.

Why is it not introduced earlier? One reason is that physical yoga—which includes breath control, special postures, and working with the body's energies—develops both power and feelings of power. The play between the feeling of power and actually being able to exert that power within ourselves can be very valuable, if handled correctly, but there are risks involved.

The feeling of power that comes from the successful practice of yoga can be used to manipulate others. Success in physical yoga can also produce pride. It takes significant effort to accomplish this kind of practice, although it's nowhere near as difficult as working directly with the mind. When, through sheer hard work, practitioners succeed in physical yoga to some degree, there is a great danger that they may become rather arrogant in the way they express themselves in the world.

I've heard it said that some traditional Tai Chi teachers develop this kind of arrogance. This is acknowledged in the Tai Chi tradition, and it seems to be a definite danger whenever there's an excessive emphasis placed on working with the body too early in the training. This is not to say that the practice of physical yoga isn't useful. If it weren't valuable, it would never have been taught as part of the Buddhist path. However, we must first go through a purifying process to remove some of our many mental trips. We need to have worked with both our own experience and with others, so that our yoga practice will genuinely benefit others as well as ourselves. That is why it isn't generally recommended early on.

Around a Single Point

Generally speaking, physical yoga works with the subtle level of the body and the channels of energy running through it. These energy channels can be disciplined, or led, by controlling the breath, in conjunction with physical movement. In Buddhist yoga this often involves a kind of dancing, as we might describe it, rather than static postures. Some aspects of this yoga are done sitting still, but others require vigorous movement.

This physical yoga is much more complicated than conventional hatha yoga, and a complete cycle of practice could take several hours. The basic idea is to connect the body to space, by combining imagery, meditation, the breath, and the physicality of the body, all in one practice.

One reason this yoga is so apparently complex, and involves so many movements and postures, is because they relate to the things we do in our everyday lives. Sometimes we sit still, while at other times we move about, and the way we do this depends on our state of mind at the time.

Practitioners train to link this practice to their everyday activities, so that when they move an arm in a particular way, for example, it suddenly connects with that same movement done in a practice environment, which links them back into a meditative experience.

When done in a sitting posture, the yoga practice uses internal physical movement to work with the breath and the subtle energy within the body. This creates a peculiar set of circumstances where we can experience aspects of the dying process while we are still alive, but without the disadvantages of sickness and mental confusion often associated with dying. By applying the technique of formless meditation to this dying process, powerful insights can arise, because the experience is much more vivid than a momentary experience surrounded by confusion or pain. Many strong insights are connected with death, simply because ego becomes more transparent, and this is another way of putting ourselves into that situation.

This practice allows us to enter and leave the dying state many times, in order to become familiar with it. While doing so, we must maintain awareness, to avoid the danger of being carried away by the experience. There wouldn't be much value in the practice if we died doing it!

Many practices at this level are about familiarizing ourselves with extreme states of mind. Yes, it's essential at first to learn ways of handling ordinary situations, but life doesn't consist only of the ordinary. We will all die at some point, plunging our minds into an extreme situation. According to Buddhist ways of thinking, we will also be reborn, which is another fairly extreme set of circumstances.

It's essential we learn to relate to circumstances where the mind becomes somewhat disconnected from the body—through illness, death, or very strong emotion. These states are equally part of life, and at this level of practice, we begin to use yoga to develop insight into such extreme situations.

What exactly is this death-like process, and why can we produce it by working with the body in this way? This is a very interesting area, where a number of very strong emotions—concerning the essence of death, sexuality, and our very existence—all come together around a single point. The yoga practice is one powerful way to experience this clearly.

More Than One Way

Those who practice at the highest level can be a bit snooty about this approach. They might say, "What do you want to do all that for? If your awareness is strong enough, you can handle any situation that arises, no matter what. You don't need a special practice to put you into extreme situations." That's true, but there is more than one way of following the path, and the practice of Buddhist yoga provides a very special and effective basis for developing awareness.

Other methods may take longer, but they don't have the attendant dangers of the physical practices. The yoga practices are best left until later in the training to ensure that any power that comes from them is not inflicted on others in an egocentric way. This is less likely if we have already begun to develop openness and compassion.

Nevertheless, it could all still go wrong. That is why, traditionally, there has always been a dialogue between the student and the teacher before these methods are taught. The teacher may decide that a student is unsuitable, or can't be sufficiently trusted, although the teacher is unlikely to put it quite so bluntly. More often, the student is told that he or she isn't ready yet and needs to wait for a while. On the other hand, the teacher might say that the student doesn't need to follow this approach at all, and will introduce him or her straightaway to the direct awareness methods used at the highest level; it just depends on the situation.

Three Levels of Yoga

In the oldest tradition of Tibetan Buddhism, the highest practice is divided into three levels. The first level uses a great deal of imagery. The second level works with the feelings and internal energies of the body by using the yoga practice described above. The third level involves working with pure awareness.

The first level—which may also include some yoga practice—works mostly with the creation of stories and legends, and uses imagery to open the mind to insight. It makes use of subtle concepts, and the various elements of the yoga practice are mostly described in symbolic terms.

For example, there is a point in one yoga practice where we realize the emptiness of our grasping at things as real. This can be so strong that we have the actual experience of everything around us being burned up and destroyed. We won't have done enough of the yoga method, at this first level, to realize this as a direct experience. Instead, we use the imagery of fire and flames. This could be presented as a story, in which there is a primordial fire, stretching through the whole of the universe, and back into time and space. If you think yourself into the story strongly enough, you become part of it, and can experience the same emptiness that comes through the yoga practice, although in a less complete fashion.

The quality of mind in space might be expressed as images of light radiating from your body, dissolving out into space. Again, there could be a storyline that expresses this process, and as the radiance returns, any sense of a solid basis to stand on also dissolves away into light and space. All you are left with is centerless space, with no central reference point. You can't find yourself in the imagery, and there is no difference between the space of your body and the space outside. Should you look for your body in this clear, vivid space, you see only swirling light. But then again, how could you look anyway, since your mind doesn't have eyes!

Another exercise would be to imagine something very complex and elaborate, but smaller than the head of a pin. Then try to see it in all its detail without zooming in. You might say, "It's much too small to see all of the details." But that is rubbish! Since we don't have eyes in our imagination, nothing can be too small. The only thing stopping us from being able to perceive all the details is the idea that it's impossible. Actually, it is quite possible; it just takes a rather long time before you can do it.

In another exercise, you attempt to step outside of yourself, turn around, and then see yourself from the front. Again, the only thing that makes this difficult is the belief that it's not possible. This exercise is actually very easy to accomplish. It's only because we don't experience such things in everyday life that it seems impossible. We extrapolate notions from the physical world into our minds, and this blocks our imagination.

There are hundreds of exercises like this, and their only purpose is to free the mind from its conceptual rigidity. They are very useful, because we are tremendously fixated on the realness of things—seen, heard, or imagined—such as size, weight, color, place, time, or any other quality that divides one thing from another.

In the world of the imagination, the only limits are self-imposed and derive from our ordinary notions about the world. It's quite irritating to realize just how much our clinging to the way things seem to work in the external world prevents us from doing things in our mind. We need to abandon those conceptual limitations, and these exercises are a good basis for doing this.

A great deal more could be said about the three highest levels of practice, especially the first level, which basically involves working with many kinds of detail in your mind. The second level uses the energies developed through physical yoga as a basis for insight. The third and final level is a direct extension of what we do in the ordinary formless sitting practice introduced right at the beginning of this book, but now it is carried to the "nth" degree. If we commit ourselves to it completely, that simple formless meditation practice can carry us to the end of the path, without the need for anything else. For most of us, however, these other practices have their place and are very useful, if not essential.

19. Tantric Alchemy

THE LIFE STORY of the Buddha tells of his encounter with the divine messengers of old age, sickness, and death. Their message is in everything we experience. At the ultimate level, these messengers connect to tantric alchemy, which is the idea that the body can be transformed, and become free from disease, ever-youthful, and undying.

However, being ever-youthful doesn't mean we never suffer from old age or death, and being free from disease doesn't mean we never get sick. So what we are talking about here? If we could be completely open to the rawness of everything we experience, we wouldn't go through periods of unconsciousness at the time of death. Because we can stand to be open and aware during the process, death is seen as just a transformation of our experience, and the same goes for birth. That's why the body is said to be undying, because when it dies, who cares?

The Continuity of Experience

When we are born, our new body is part of that continuity of experience, so it's like we have a continuous body. And it's the same for youth and old age. Externally, we may appear to get old, but internally we remain ever youthful, like Manjushri, the great bodhisattva of wisdom, who is also called Manjushri Kumarabhuta, "Ever-Youthful Manjushri."

The same continuity applies to sickness and health. When great teach-ers like Longchen Rabjam became sick or old, they were said to exhibit "the phenomena of sickness" or "the phenomena of old age." Reading this, it's easy to think, "These are weasel words if ever there were! They're trying to get around the fact that he got sick and died like anyone else." In fact, it's just a way of indicating that great practitioners reach the stage where old age, sickness, and death aren't experienced in an ordinary way but as part of this continuity of experience.

At that point, they demonstrate such phenomena simply for the benefit of others. Even Buddha Shakyamuni exhibited the phenomena of birth and death, it is said, so that we wouldn't ever think that birth and death are just a game.

20. As the Path Unfolds

ONE WAY to look at the Buddhist path would be to imagine how it would unfold for the perfect practitioner. Of course, there are few such practitioners, but this allows us to look at our own path and see what obstacles and difficulties may arise, and the corrective measures we could take to overcome them. We can assume that we will experience difficulties on the path, and that with the help of a teacher, we will find a way through them.

For many of us, our first inspiration to practice comes in response to those basic questions about the nature of existence that arise from ordinary experience. As our meditation practice deepens, a creeping sense of uncertainty arises in what seems to be the center of our lives, as ego is revealed to be insecure and easily collapsed.

Eventually we come to some realization of non-self. This is a big event, to say the least. Unfortunately, it is unlikely to last forever, unless we are very remarkable practitioners. Through understanding the emptiness of self, and by working with the emotional problems that go along with this realization, our egocentricity is greatly reduced. But despite this knowledge, the actual experience will come and go, and emotionally speaking, we retain a strong—though not as solid—sense of self.

However much our teachers tell us to practice without focusing on attainment, an element of goal orientation is inevitably involved. Even speaking in terms of a path suggests that it goes somewhere, and so we practice to achieve a goal, rather than for its own sake. Consequently, we approach the Dharma, the most valuable thing in our lives, in the same ambitious way we seek good jobs, security, and worldly success. It's essentially the same goal-driven approach but directed toward the spiritual sphere, the sacred world of Dharma. The style is the same, and that ambition shapes the end we have in view.

The truth of this is fairly obvious. It's been recognized as an obstacle for thousands of years, and is one of the classic problems faced on the Buddhist path. While the more obvious goal orientation may diminish over time, ambition persists at the center of our practice. To see this clearly is the next big event in our lives as Dharma practitioners.

A Much Wider Vision

Why do we still stumble into these traps despite knowing they are there? The reason is that our understanding remains at an intellectual level. It's not enough just to be told about the deadliness of ambition. We need to directly experience the completeness of our folly—to realize how truly poisonous it is—before we can let go of it. We have to see it for ourselves.

The thrust of ambition is to attain something, and even those genuine efforts to understand and realize the Dharma are subtly skewed toward our own benefit. In the beginning, this isn't such a problem. Eventually, however, it is that stamp of ego that taints everything we do and twists it into something deadly. It's only once we vomit up this ambitious way of being, like poisoned meat, that the next great level of understanding can arise.

At this point on the path, we develop a much wider vision, and a genuine lack of self-interest begins to arise. We stop thinking so much in terms of our own benefit, and it becomes genuinely meaningful to talk about valuing others as much as ourselves. This is a pivotal moment in our understanding. Only when we have begun to drop our strongly held concepts about the world can the powers of a bodhisattva develop, enabling us to transform situations for ourselves and others. Our worldview becomes empowered, and genuine wisdom and compassion come to the fore in our lives.

We begin the path by recognizing that there is something to discover, and that we have the power to discover it. Now we realize that for this discovery to be complete, it must benefit others as well as ourselves, and even go beyond the very idea of self and other. This is unquestionably the greatest path to follow.

The Greater Path

This path is the Mahayana, the great way of the bodhisattva. It begins with a genuine inspiration to give up attachment to self-interest and ambition. With that comes an intuition of the ungraspability, not only of self, but also of everything connected with the sensory world and the mind.

As our view of the world changes, it becomes possible to love others in a way that we previously reserved for ourselves alone. This genuine love is self-existent, beyond all contrivance and manipulation. It arises spontaneously, simply because the obstacles to its arising have been removed. Consequently, we can't command this to happen. Trying to do so only results in another experience constructed out of ambition and ego-centricity. Furthermore, genuinely compassionate activity goes beyond any sense of limitation. Even thinking that love, compassion, and joy should be restricted to sentient beings can become a form of clinging.

We talked earlier about the sense of well-being that arises through our practice. This grows as we follow the path. Eventually it is revealed as an inherent part of what we are, rather than something "in here" or "out there." And we can act from that position of natural well-being, benefiting others without fear, because it is so constant. In the beginning, our sense of love, joy, compassion, and well-being is related to specific beings. Eventually, well-being and compassion become part of the way our senses operate, and we experience them in all situations, whether others are present or not.

Ordinarily, our knowledge of other people remains superficial, even when we're well acquainted. We know their physical appearance and the kinds of things they're likely to say or do in certain circumstances. If we're very close, we may have some notion about how they think and the way their emotions operate. But they can always surprise us; indeed, we can always surprise ourselves, because something is always going on below the surface, or beyond the horizon, as it were.

Ordinarily, what we know about another person is analogous to those small, isolated islands in the Pacific. They appear to be tiny rocks, separated by vast oceans, but on further investigation we find they are the tips of great mountains arising from the same underlying bedrock. From the Buddhist point of view, the basic nature of all beings is vast in much the same way. What we see is just the superficial mountaintop.

As our understanding deepens, we get the opportunity to see more of the possibilities that lie hidden in other people, in an almost intuitive way. We can resonate with them, bringing out qualities that seem impossible to imagine now, and the deeper we go into Dharma, the more significant this becomes.

Finally, we go beyond the subtleties of the senses and the objects of awareness to see the nature of awareness itself. There is an intrinsic lucency or clarity in the nature of awareness that lies at the heart of compassion, joy, and the ungraspable spaciousness of non-ego. Now, whenever we look within, we glimpse the ungraspable nature of what we are. Looking without, we see that same ungraspability in others. A much vaster vision of the nature of sentient beings arises.

Bodhisattvas respond to the vastness of other beings and can inspire them to respond to their own vastness as well, but only within certain limits. The Buddha had realized this perfectly, so why didn't everyone he met become enlightened? It is sad to realize that even the awakened ones can only do so much. Each of us has our own confusion, which cannot be removed entirely by another or entirely through our own awareness. The Buddhist path is a mixture of helping ourselves and working with others, and we need to have both.

21. Beginning at the End

W E EACH INHABIT our own personal world of confusion and karmic conditioning. Fortunately for us, awakening can occasionally break through that conditioned sphere. Otherwise, it would be hopeless, and we would be forever bound by confusion, with no hope of freedom.

Unfortunately our karmic conditioning doesn't disappear the instant we start out on the Buddhist path. For most people, the breakthrough of what is real happens gradually. The speed and manner of this process depends partly on our individual karmic conditioning. That is why some people can meditate for forty or fifty years without anything seeming to happen, while other practitioners apparently achieve breakthroughs almost spontaneously. Our conditioning determines the shape of the opening through which reality can emerge.

Through Dirty Spectacles

It would be a very unfortunate person who had such powerful conditioning that nothing could ever break through. However, some people are so strongly fixed in their ideas and habits that they are best advised to concentrate on performing good actions rather than trying to cultivate insight. In this way they develop punya. This will bear fruit later on as a kind of opening, one that may enable them to meet a teacher who can help them in a more direct way.

Through the power of compassion and bodhichitta, buddhas and great bodhisattvas, free from karmic conditioning, appear in the world in order to help us. Because we view them through our karmic conditioning, however, we don't see them as they really are. We see them rather through dirty spectacles, and they may not appear remarkably enlightened as a result. Though they manifest through the power of bodhichitta, they do so in a form especially helpful to the beings concerned, and in that sense their appearance is narrowed and limited. But their forms are actually finely tuned tools for doing a particular job in a particular time and place.

We could say that Buddha Shakyamuni appeared as he did for the sake of the people of India at that particular time. But the Dharma he taught was later transmitted to many places and cultures, and now people throughout the world have access to it.

Advanced bodhisattvas are people on the path like us, but more toward the other end of the spectrum. They still have karmic conditioning, but they have the power to use it to put themselves into particular times and places to help others. They also use the fact that reality breaks through their karmic conditioning more easily to wear their conditioning away while helping others at the same time.

As ordinary practitioners, we find ourselves somewhat at the mercy of our conditioning and have to work with it as best we can. With the help of the buddhas and bodhisattvas, we begin to get flashes of insight, which we can then use to help ourselves and others. In this way we, too, become beginner bodhisattvas.

Just the Beginning

Having gone this far, we might think we've reached the end of the path. Not so! It is actually just the beginning. We may have transformed our bodies and gained the ability to create enormous power, influence, and emotional transformation, but as they say in the traditional texts, we are still on the "path of training"!

I once asked Trungpa Rinpoche about this: "Surely this is enlighten-ment." To which he replied, "Oh no! This is just the start. It is where you begin, not where you end." It is a bit of a shaker to realize that despite having gone so far, we have merely dipped our toes in the water. Now we must travel across the sea.

Another teacher said that even after a certain great realization, we could remain on the path of training for thousands of kalpas, which is untold millions of years. But why would we care? From that moment on, every-thing we do develops punya, compassion, and further insight.

The path lasts for an extremely long time because our ability to act must develop in vast and incredible ways, literally beyond anything we can imagine. It must mirror the vastness of the universe itself. Only at the end of this process do we reach "non-training" and the end of the path.

The Way of Truth

We start with our fundamental questions, believing there is a truth to be discovered, and that human beings have the capacity to reveal it. As we go on, we realize that the qualities of openness and clarity are not only integral to the nature of truth, they are also the means we use to discover it. In this sense, the truth itself is the way.

It's like a voyage of discovery, in which we work with our natural con-nection to truth, the sense of its nearness, and the compelling power it possesses. It is because this truth is already within our being that those basic questions arise in the first place.

The goal is to reveal that truth completely, and because the nature of reality and the truth are not separate, to discover the truth is to realize the nature of reality itself. The search for truth is not just about realizing the nature of the universe around us. It is also a journey to reveal what we truly are. It's about discovering our awe-inspiring nature, which is hid-den beneath the surface, like precious ore concealed in mountains. The coming together of the truth that seems to be internal and the truth that seems to be external is compassionate bodhichitta.

Bodhichitta is the absolute union of wisdom and compassion. It is the heart of awakening and the truth of the path. Through the practice of bodhichitta, we ourselves become the truth. We become the answer to all our questions and an expression of awakening in the world, for the sake of ourselves and others. At that point the path is complete. We have accomplished everything we needed to do and have become an awakened one.

Of course there is no end to the activity of bodhichitta, because it connects us to all those beings who search for truth, whether or not they have found it. It also links us to the limitless beings who have never asked these questions, who live and die in little more than a mechanical fashion, but have the potential to be so much more.

The Best Advice

We talk about the path taking many millions of years to complete. On the other hand, it doesn't take long to reach the point of irreversibility. And there are many ways of practicing that telescope this process—even, it is said, into one lifetime.

The slow and steady path lasts a very long time but has fewer dangers associated with it. The quicker path is definitely more dangerous. Having said that, it isn't as if we have a choice. It is a question of meeting the right teacher, and having the right connections. Even then there are differences, because some of us have sharper faculties than others. So there is a short-short path, a long-short path, and many gradations in between.

Certain Buddhist texts suggest we can reach irreversibility, if not enlightenment, in a single day. Some people apparently became enlightened within seconds of meeting the Buddha. It is inspiring to think this might be true. But taking this approach could make our practice frenetic and pressured. The danger is we become so goal-oriented and heavy on ourselves that we can't practice properly.

When practitioners feel they can become enlightened in record time, they push themselves very hard and spend a lot of time looking for enlightened teachers to learn from. But giving ourselves a hard time is always a mistake—and how would we recognize an awakened person if we met one?

The best advice is to forget about trying to attain anything and just practice as best you can. Find a teacher you can relate to and work with whatever strength you have, without becoming frenetic. That is all you have to do. As Trungpa Rinpoche used to say, "Just keep on sitting! Keep on sitting, and you will realize it in the end."

Glossary

anitya (Sanskrit). Impermanence and change, a key quality of samsara.

avidya (Sanskrit). Ignorance of the true nature of reality.

adhisthana (Sanskrit). Often translated as "blessing," but more the idea of being possessed by the presence and influence of awakening. The sustaining or transforming power of Dharma transmission.

bodhichitta (Sanskrit). The awakened heart and mind; involves both the mental qualities of intelligence and clarity, and the heart qualities of love and compassion.

bodhisattva (Sanskrit). Someone training to arouse bodhichitta in him- or herself in order to become awakened for the benefit of others.

buddha (Sanskrit). "Awakened one"; a being who has realized enlightenment, such as Shakyamuni, the historical Buddha.

Buddhadharma (Sanskrit). The teaching or way of the Buddha.

Dharma (Sanskrit). As used here, Dharma is the teaching of the Buddha, including all the many meditation methods and views used in the tradition. More deeply, it refers to the awakened qualities that are revealed by following the path.

duhkha (Sanskrit). Normally translated as "suffering," but actually a much broader term that implies the whole spectrum of unsatisfactory and frustrating experience, ranging from the most intense and claustrophobic pain to the most subtle sense of incompleteness; the first of the four noble truths.

dzogchen (Tibetan) or *maha-ati* (Sanskrit). "The great perfection"; the highest teaching of the Buddha according to the oldest tradition of Tibetan Buddhism (the Nyingma tradition.)

dzogrim (Tibetan). Completion- or perfection-stage meditation in Buddhist tantra; more generally, the formless aspect of meditation.

jnanasambhara (Sanskrit). The accumulation of insight, or awareness.

kalpa (Sanskrit). An eon; a vast period of time.

karma (Sanskrit). "Action"; generally, activity arising from ignorance, desire, and hatred that leads to relatively happy or miserable states of existence; not to be confused with *buddha karma* which is awakened activity, free from confusion.

klesha (Sanskrit). Negative emotion or mental poison. Hatred, desire, and ignorance are the three fundamental kleshas.

kyerim (Tibetan). Development-stage meditation in Buddhist tantra, and more generally any practice that emphasizes the form aspect.

mahamudra (Sanskrit). "The great symbol"; the highest teaching of Buddhist tantra according to the later wave of Tibetan Buddhist schools.

Mahayana (Sanskrit). The "great way" or "great vehicle" of the bodhisattva, leading to the complete awakening of a buddha.

mala (Sanskrit). A garland of beads used for counting mantras and other practices.

mandala (Sanskrit). Literally "round" or "circular," but here it refers to the dynamic general principle through which everything manifests.

Key elements of a mandala include the central principle, a related periphery, and a boundary.

mantra (Sanskrit). Awakened speech in the form of Sanskrit syllables that are repeated or chanted. Practitioners can link into the world and milieu of a great bodhisattva or buddha by repeating his or her mantra.

marga (Sanskrit). The "path" that leads to the cessation of suffering—fourth of the four noble truths.

maya (Sanskrit). Illusion, the misleading appearances that distract us from seeing the true nature of reality.

nirodha (Sanskrit). The "cessation" of suffering—third of the four noble truths.

prajna (Sanskrit). Wisdom or intelligence; the faculty to discern truth in our experience, and the wisdom we discover.

pranidhana (Sanskrit) or *monlam* (Tibetan). Aspiration or intention made by bodhisattvas to benefit others.

punya (Sanskrit). Often translated as "merit," punya is the power and influence that arises from all wholesome and skillful action, especially Dharma activity.

punyasambhara (Sanskrit). The accumulation of punya.

rimé (Tibetan). "Unbiased"; a great nonsectarian movement in nineteenth-century Tibet that helped revive many declining lineages of Buddhist practice.

samsara (Sanskrit). Conditioned existence; the wheel of birth and death, driven by ignorance, desire, and hatred, and characterized by *duhkha*, or suffering.

samaya (Sanskrit). "Bond" or "connection"; in Buddhist tantra, the powerful bond between student and teacher. More generally, the connections between different elements of a mandala.

samudaya (Sanskrit). The "cause" of suffering—second of the four noble truths.

satori (Japanese). Zen Buddhist term for realization beyond thought.

skandha (Sanskrit). Literally "heap" or "aggregate." The five skandhas of form, feeling, perception, formations, and consciousness make up the experience of a human being.

tantra (Sanskrit). Texts and yogic practices used in the Vajrayana, the "indestructible vehicle."

From the Editor

THE TEACHINGS in this book are taken from Rigdzin Shikpo's "Heart Essence" course, which was designed to give new students a flavor of the approach followed in his teaching mandala, the Longchen Foundation, as well as an introduction to formless meditation.

Running through all the teachings in this book is a strong emphasis on working with direct experience, both in formal meditation sessions and in daily life. Buddhist meditation is never practiced in isolation from a view of some kind. It is the view that gives a sense of direction and provides a source of inspiration for the practice. In the approach Rigdzin Shikpo presents here, the view and meditation are very closely related, and it is difficult to talk about the vision aspect without giving some details of the associated meditative technique. Consequently these pages contain not only a full account of the basic formless meditation, but also a description of other methods that can be used to undermine the seeming solidity of such things as time and place, and ways of linking into the wisdom aspect of negative emotions.

It would be a mistake to think that the instructions given here are sufficient in themselves, for it just isn't possible to learn meditation from a book, however inspiring. Buddhist practice works in terms of transmission, which in its most basic form means that we need to receive the inspiration of the view and the meditative techniques directly from another person for them to be of any deeper value. Rigdzin Shikpo, echoing

Trungpa Rinpoche, often says that there is no such thing as a "self-made" man or woman in Buddhism. For our meditation to be truly meaningful, we need to work with a teacher and a mandala of fellow practitioners, who provide the encouragement, support, and direct feedback that ensures our practice develops in the right way, for the benefit of both ourselves and others.

About Rigdzin Shikpo

Rigdzin Shikpo (as Michael Hookham) first came into contact with Buddhism as a young school boy in the 1940s, when his class read an otherwise conventional boy's adventure story set in Thailand. The story contained, as one of its chapters, the life of the Buddha up to his renunciation of palace life. Rigdzin Shikpo was tremendously inspired by the Buddha's story and his self-sacrifice for all beings, but it was not until much later, as a student in the 1950s, that he had the practical opportunity to find out more about the Buddha's teaching.

Rigdzin Shikpo first studied and practiced Buddhism under the guidance of Western monks in the Theravadan tradition, which is prevalent today in Thailand and Sri Lanka. Later he followed the path of the bodhisattva in the Mahayana tradition, which flourished in ancient India and continued into modern times in Tibet and East Asia. Then, in 1965, he met the young Tibetan exile Trungpa Rinpoche.

Chögyam Trungpa Rinpoche was the eleventh incarnation in the Trungpa line and the abbot of Surmang Monastery in Eastern Tibet. Rinpoche, who was a lineage holder in both the Nyingma and Kagyü traditions of Tibetan Buddhism, had been forced to flee his homeland following the Chinese takeover of Tibet in 1959. A vivid account of his early life and dramatic escape can be found in his autobiography, *Born in Tibet*. Having spent several years living in India, Trungpa Rinpoche came to study at Oxford University in the early 1960s.

In 1965 Rigdzin Shikpo, with his Dharma brother Alf Vial, went to visit Trungpa Rinpoche privately in Oxford. They presented him with several Tibetan texts they had acquired, one of which was from the tradition of Guru Rinpoche, or Padmasambhava, the great Indian yogin who introduced Vajrayana Buddhism into Tibet in the eighth century.

It turned out that this text was something quite special to Trungpa Rinpoche, and he decided, on the spot, to start teaching the practices contained within it. Over the months and years that followed, Rinpoche trained the two Englishmen in both the preliminary and main practices of dzogchen, or *maha-ati* as he called it, the innermost teachings of the Nyingma tradition, the oldest of the four great schools of Tibetan Buddhism. It was during this time that Trungpa Rinpoche gave Rigdzin Shikpo special teaching on the dzogchen view, some of which has recently been published in volume 1 of Trungpa Rinpoche's collected works under the title, "The Way of Maha Ati."

These days there are abundant books and opportunities to train in Tibetan Buddhist practice, and it is difficult now to imagine quite how rare it was to encounter such teachings only a few decades ago. Rigdzin Shikpo talked about his early experiences and first encounters with Trungpa Rinpoche in an afterword he wrote for a British edition of *Born in Tibet* published in the 1980s:

> My first adult meeting with Buddhism took place in the early 1950s. The teachings of non-self and emptiness had the impelling force of revelation, and as I read further and learnt something of Tibetan Buddhism I felt that further vistas were unfolding.
>
> In particular, after reading scattered references to the "Heart Essence of Longchen" in various books I felt a sense of grief and recognition. The recognition was like encountering again a world of great profundity and vast vision that had been forgotten; the grief was the fact of its total inaccessibility—no texts, no teachers, no way of entering the path. At that time there seemed to be no prospect whatsoever of any real encounter with the Buddhism of Tibet. The only thing one could do was to work as genuinely as possible with the Dharma available and the sense of longing for the heart essence teachings themselves.

However, in a manner totally unforeseen, the teachings of Tibetan Buddhism came to the West. The great national tragedy of the Tibetan people was the means by which teachers and teachings alike became widely available to aspiring Western practitioners and probably saved Tibetan Buddhism from eventual extinction as a living tradition....

Trungpa Rinpoche was one of the teachers who successfully escaped from Tibet and came to teach in the West, initially in Oxford. It was there that a friend and I met him and took our first steps under his guidance. After having practised for over ten years without the thought that such a relationship would ever be possible, meeting Rinpoche and working with him seemed a miraculous event. His teaching of natural perfection, openness and spontaneity helped us in cutting attachment to the Dharma as personal property.

At this point the personal significance of Rinpoche's teaching begins to merge with a wider, more general significance. He was the first to introduce the living tradition of Tibetan Buddhism to Britain, and since we had no other ways with which to compare it, we did not realize that Rinpoche taught and prepared us more in the style of the older tradition of India and Tibet than in the new....

Rigdzin Shikpo sometimes talks about Trungpa Rinpoche as the "Western Padmakara." Padmakara, another name for Guru Rinpoche, introduced the Dharma into Tibet in the face of very considerable resistance from local forces who were hostile to Buddhist culture. It seems significant that Trungpa Rinpoche began his teaching in the West by introducing the Guru Padmakara tradition in Britain.

The Longchen Foundation

In 1970 Trungpa Rinpoche left Britain to live in the United States, and Rigdzin Shikpo continued to take teachings and transmissions from

Rinpoche, visiting him until Rinpoche's death in 1987. Trungpa Rinpoche also encouraged Rigdzin Shikpo to study with one of his own principal teachers, Dilgo Khyentse Rinpoche.

It was with the encouragement and blessing of the two Rinpoches and growing out of the original "*Chö* Group" (Dharma Group) started with Trungpa Rinpoche's blessing in 1968 that the Longchen Foundation was established in 1975. Its name arose from Trungpa Rinpoche's special feeling for what he called, "the unique Dharma logic of Longchen Rabjam," the great fourteenth-century Nyingma master. This way of teaching and meditating Rinpoche saw as crucial to the West, and he entrusted Rigdzin Shikpo to realize the vision and to pass on this vision to others. This is the tradition of Mahayana maha-ati, in which the whole of the path is simultaneously and completely pervaded by both the compassionate heart of Mahayana and the view of maha-ati.

Rigdzin Shikpo established deep Dharma connections with other Tibetan teachers as well, most especially Dudjom Rinpoche, Khamtrul Yeshe Dorje Rinpoche, and Khenpo Tsultrim Gyamtso Rinpoche. Khenpo Rinpoche became Rigdzin Shikpo's principal source of guidance following the deaths of Trungpa Rinpoche and Dilgo Khyentse Rinpoche.

Khenpo Tsultrim Gyamtso Rinpoche is both a very learned scholar and a highly accomplished yogin, and he furthered the teachings that Trungpa Rinpoche had given. It was under Khenpo Rinpoche's personal supervision that Rigdzin Shikpo undertook a three-year solitary retreat in 1990. One unusual feature of this retreat was that it took place in an otherwise ordinary semi-detached house, in an urban setting.

Following the successful accomplishment of this retreat, Khenpo Rinpoche gave Michael Hookham the title Rigdzin Shikpo, authorized him to teach the full path of the Nyingma tradition to his students, and declared the Longchen Foundation to be a Buddhist school in its own right.

In 2002 Rigdzin Shikpo established the "Lion's Roar," a three-year introductory training taught over nine weekends, or "gates." The heart of the Lion's Roar is formless meditation and the path of openness and awareness. For more details about the Lion's Roar program please see the Longchen Foundation website: longchenfoundation.com.

Acknowledgments

I must start by thanking Rigdzin Shikpo for his generosity in making these teachings available, firstly to his personal students, and now to a wider audience, through the publication of this book. He has shown great confidence in entrusting me with the task of editing his spoken words, and I take full responsibility for any inadvertent errors or distortions that may have come about through the editorial process.

Secondly, I must acknowledge the very considerable contribution of Helen Berliner, whose professional editorial expertise has helped to transform my original manuscript into the book you are reading.

Special thanks are due to Nick Rimmer and Louise Marchant, who transcribed and checked the original talks on which this book is based. Thanks are also due to my Dharma brothers and sisters in the Longchen community, in particular Tim Malnick, Steve Hinde, and Sally Sheldrake, for their help in getting the whole project started.

This book would not have seen the light of day without the support—in every sense—and encouragement of my partner, Caroline Cupitt. Finally, I would also like to thank my commissioning editor, David Kittelstrom from Wisdom Publications, for his encouragement over the several years that have elapsed since we first began talking about this project.

David Hutchens (Urgyen Dawa)
London, England, April 2007

Index

About Wisdom Publications

W ISDOM PUBLICATIONS, a nonprofit publisher, is dedicated to making available authentic works relating to Buddhism for the benefit of all. We publish books by ancient and modern masters in all traditions of Buddhism, translations of important texts, and original scholarship. Additionally, we offer books that explore East-West themes unfolding as traditional Buddhism encounters our modern culture in all its aspects. Our titles are published with the appreciation of Buddhism as a living philosophy, and with the special commitment to preserve and transmit important works from Buddhism's many traditions.

To learn more about Wisdom, or to browse books online, visit our website at www.wisdompubs.org.

You may request a copy of our catalog online or by writing to this address:

Wisdom Publications
199 Elm Street
Somerville, Massachusetts 02144 USA
Telephone: 617-776-7416 ✦ Fax: 617-776-7841
Email: info@wisdompubs.org ✦ www.wisdompubs.org

The Wisdom Trust

As a nonprofit publisher, Wisdom is dedicated to the publication of Dharma books for the benefit of all sentient beings and dependent upon the kindness and generosity of sponsors in order to do so. If you would like to make a donation to Wisdom, you may do so through our website or our Somerville office. If you would like to help sponsor the publication of a book, please write or email us at the address above.

Thank you.

Wisdom is a nonprofit, charitable 501(c)(3) organization affiliated with the Foundation for the Preservation of the Mahayana Tradition (FPMT).

Saying Yes to Life (Even the Hard Parts)
Ezra Bayda with Josh Bartok
Foreword by Thomas Moore
272 pages, ISBN 0-86171-274-9, $15.00

"You can live with this book like a friend or a spouse— not necessarily in absolute harmony, but in real engagement. I already have my favorite pages, sayings that I don't want to forget, formulations that are clearly inspired. How many books give you that much?"—from the foreword by Thomas Moore, bestselling author of *Care of the Soul*

Awakening Through Love
Unveiling Your Deepest Goodness
John Makransky
Foreword by Lama Surya Das
288 pp, ISBN 0-86171-537-3, $16.95

"*Awakening Through Love* is a root text in a lineage of applied social intelligence, offering practical methods for cultivating empathy and compassion—not in some remote mountain hermitage, but in the midst of life. Makransky's wisdom will benefit anyone who yearns to become more loving."—Daniel Goleman, author of *Social Intelligence*